*For my wife Jenny, the love of my life and the rock I lean on for support in all of my endeavors big and small;*

*For my son Ethan, my little munchkin who completed my life and never fails to put a smile on my face;*

*For my parents who always supported my golfing passion as well as the rest of my life;*

*For the golfers on the PGA Tour, they are the best golfers in the world and even they don't hit every shot pure every time; and*

*For all of the duffers out there for whom this book was written...you are not alone.*

# 1. YOU ARE NOT ALONE

It is March 23, 2008. For the time being, it is a dry day in Doral, Florida, but the rain that will be starting in an hour or so causes a steady wind. A golfer steps to the tee on a difficult par-3. Water and a bunker guard the front and the water also is a mere 10 feet to the left of the green. Naturally, the flag is only a few feet from the left edge of the green and just over the bunker. There is room right, but a good, and obviously brave, golfer trying to make birdie can hit a solid iron at the flag. The wind is blowing from the golfer's left to right, so a slight miss might be held up by the wind.

Taking dead aim at the flag, he prepared for the aggressive shot over the water, over the bunker and at the pin. His takeaway was perfect, but as he began the transition into his downswing something caught his attention. He pulled his shot left, and if not for the wind, he most certainly would have landed in the water along the left side. Immediately after completing his follow-through, this golfer snapped, blaming the source for his miscue.

Most, if not all, of the people who read this book have experienced a similar scenario. However, this situation is slightly different because the golfer in question happened to be one of the greatest, if not the greatest, golfers the world has ever known: Tiger Woods. The source of the distraction was a photographer who snapped a picture just as Tiger began his transition. While Tiger's "mishit" landed in the rough a few feet off of the green, we must remember that he is a phenom. Undoubtedly for us humans that shot would have landed in the water, traveled 100 feet in front of us or maybe not even rolled off of the tee box.

The point is, even the best golfer in the world can be distracted during a shot, have an off hole or even a substandard round. Unfortunately for 99.9% of the population, we do not have the luxury of blaming a photographer snapping a picture during a World Golf Championship event. So, for the rest of us, I have compiled a list of (mostly) plausible excuses.

These excuses range from the mundane to the insane. But they all serve as excuses that you should feel free to use the next time your game is not cooperating. Instead of worrying about keeping your head down or having a smooth follow through, break out this handy tool and blame something else, anything else. Because remember, we cannot play like Tiger Woods, even if we do wear the same clothes he does.

## 2. BEFORE YOU GET TO THE GOLF COURSE

Many golfers believe that they have to wait until they are at the course before they can start searching for excuses. This is a common mistake amongst amateur excuse-making golfers. In fact, nothing could be farther from the truth. Proper preparation for doling out excuses can begin the night before your round, and in some extreme cases, even earlier.

### A. I Had a Long Night Last Night

One of my close friends from high school was getting married, so we decided to hold his bachelor party in Atlantic City. Before getting to the hotel that Saturday, we scheduled golf at a county course. I was not staying over in Atlantic City Saturday night, so I decided to get all of my weekend's imbibing accomplished on Friday night. Having arrived at my bed close to 3 A.M., I laid my spinning head down on the pillow and the next thing I knew my alarm was blaring. Equipped with my clubs and a change of clothes for dinner, and of course, a massive headache, I headed out to play in 85 degree heat.

Playing in hot weather is never easy (see Chapter 3.B), but playing with a hangover in hot weather, well that is just silliness. Things started off okay, I saved bogey after driving my tee shot through the fairway and having to pitch out backwards just to have a shot at the green. From there, we headed out into the sun and things went from okay to bad to really bad fairly quickly. A drive down the middle was followed by an approach shot that might have made the green had I not nearly passed out mid-swing. A bit queasy, I delicately played a 60 foot bump and run; the only problem was that the hole was 30 feet away. Another chip and three putts later and I knew that it was going to be a long LONG day. Somewhere around the 8$^{th}$ hole I stopped counting my strokes and started counting how many times I thought I was having a stroke. Thankfully, and mercifully, the course was empty so our three foursomes joined together for a back-nine alternate shot competition.

The majority of that round, as well as the rest of the day, was spent regaling my compatriots with tales of my drinking prowess from the night before. They may have simply thought I was sharing stories for fun, but I made sure to end each rendition with the same thought: "…and that's why I played like crap today."

So, whether you have gone on an all day bender, stayed out a little later than normal or simply had one drink with dinner, the lesson here is: do not be afraid to blame your prior night's activities for a poor round of golf.

B.        *Who Could Sleep With All That Noise*

Never underestimate the value of a good night's sleep. Truer words may never have been spoken. We have all had our share of nights when the pillow does not feel right, the room is too hot or too cold, our significant other is too close or maybe a storm keeps us up all night with loud cracks of thunder and eye-popping lightening. Each one of these can cause tired swings or a lack of concentration. Never be afraid to utilize these excuses at any point during your round.

While the above are justified excuses any of us can use, all of them pale in comparison to the havoc a new born child wreaks. Every parent I have ever spoken to has informed me that having a child is the greatest thing that could happen to you. Of course, these are the same people that will tell you to enjoy your freedom because once you have kids your life is not your own anymore. I can tell you from my own experience, both of these statements are 100 percent true.

Used to sleeping through the night? Forget about it. Used to sleeping in on the weekends? Ha, not anymore. Used to playing a round of golf with your eyes open for the entire round? Not a shot. But, instead of letting that lack of sleep frustrate you, use it as a positive. When you fall asleep in your cart during your next round, just blame your baby.

Over the summers I play at a very nice semi-private course in Little Egg Harbor, NJ, called Sea Oaks. Having played there for several years and become friendly with most of the employees, I am able to secure the first or second tee time every Saturday during the summer. There is truly nothing better than teeing off at 6:00 A.M.

and playing in 3 hours (plus, you can always use your early tee time as an excuse, "It is so early I feel like I am still sleeping").

One morning, while I was paying my greens fees, someone called the course at around 5:30 A.M. to see if he could get a tee time for that morning. The guy behind the counter said sure, as long as the caller could be at the course in time to tee off at 6:08 A.M. (my tee time). I do not remember his name, but I do remember that he looked a bit out of sorts.

As we played we began talking about our lives. His wife had recently delivered their first child. How long ago was recently, I asked. Three days ago! Turns out that this guy was up all night with his newborn and figured once he got the kid to sleep he would see if he could get a quick round of golf in before the kid woke up. Needless to say, I was astonished. Not because his wife let him out (a miraculous feat in and of itself), but because by his account he had not slept for more than a few hours for each of the past three nights. He said he was an 11-handicap. He played okay, finishing somewhere in the neighborhood of a 98-99. With every bad shot he reminded me that he had just had a kid (women, this excuse works even better for you).

The moral here: having kids affords you yet another excuse for a poor round. After all, your kids are going to blame you for things throughout their entire life, you might as well do the same.

C.  *It's Been a While*

Other than you retired folks who live in golf country year round and can play whenever you choose, most of us cannot get to the links with consistency. What most amateur golfers fail to recognize is the impenetrable excuse this provides. Sure some people can practice during the off-season, but most of us are simply resigned to memories, putting on the carpet and imaginary swings in the elevator.

My parents have a house in Florida, so for one week during the winter my wife and I head down to the Sunshine State for relaxation and, for me, non-stop golf. Inevitably, this trip takes place after a several month layoff. Among the items I pack for this trip, I always make sure to include my bag of excuses. "It's been 5 months since I last golfed." "I am not worried about my score, I am just trying to get the feel of my swing back." Or, "Of course you beat me, you get to play every day, while some of us have jobs and responsibilities." My father especially likes that last one.

This excuse also serves you well for your first, or even second, round of the season. While walking up to the first tee, do not be afraid to tell your playing partners that this is the first time you are getting out this season. A little comment such as, "Wow, it feels good to finally be back out on a golf course" or "I just want to get some feel back" should do the trick. That said, there is no problem busting out the "This is my first round of the season, so I hope I remember how to swing a club." Then, every time you hit a good shot you can follow it up with "Now that is how I was hitting everything at the end of last year."

D.     *A Funny Thing Happened on the Way to the Course*

Many professional golfers have worked with sports psychologists over the years. One of the common techniques professional golfers use is visualization. Essentially, the night before a tournament, a professional golfer will imagine each shot of the next day's round in his or her head. They then take that mental image with them the next day and try to execute those images.

I believe this is a great technique for every golfer. It helps heighten your ability to concentrate, as well as allow you to get over bad shots more quickly. However, the key to this technique is to maintain focus for the entire round. Golf is a constant mental battle and you must concentrate. This leads us to our next excuse.

With the ever increasing number of cars on the road, there is a strong probability that you saw an accident, almost got into an accident, got pulled over or even had car trouble on your way to the course. Any of these occurrences could have caused you to lose concentration. I know several times I have mentally pictured a solid round of 68 or

69, only to end up shooting an 87. Rather than blame that 3-putt from 10 feet, it is easier to switch focus to what happened on your way to the course that caused the break in concentration that eventually led to the 3-putt.

At this stage, it is imperative that you remember golf is a game of creativity and adaptability. If you drove with your partner to the course, or worse, your partner picked you up from your house, blaming something that happened during the drive will not fly. In such a scenario, remember that your friend does not live with you. How does he know what happened to you while you were getting your clubs out of the trunk of your car or while you were patiently waiting to be picked up?

Allow me to illustrate my point using an example from one of my mother's friends. My mom and her friend Beth were scheduled to play a round together. Since Beth's house was on the way to the course, my mom was going to drive. After putting her clubs in the trunk and getting into the car, Beth immediately dove into her excuse. "I might not have a great round today. You're not going to believe what just happened."

Well it turns out that Beth was having some garage door trouble, as in it would not open (if I have learned anything through my marriage, I can safely say that this was no doubt her husband's fault). Now most people would have simply taken the clubs out of the car and gone out the front door. Not Beth. She decided to manually lift the garage door. And, as one would naturally expect, the door did not stay in place and came down on her head. Since she had only lifted it high enough to get out, the door did not cause injury or trauma. Rather, it caused just enough pain to knock the vision of her game out of her head. Damn garage doors, they will get you every time.

The lesson here is that anything can break your concentration and throw your entire day off even before you take your first practice swing on the driving range. The experienced golfer always keeps his eyes on the ball, but has good enough peripheral vision to spot a possible excuse and exploit it during his round.

3.   BAD CONDITIONS

Weather is an extremely important part of golf. A slight change in wind direction or speed can alter club selection, distance control or even blow hair into your eyes. When the weather turns colder your ball will not travel as far, and of course, you cannot play as much so the need for excuses tends to increase.

An experienced golfer has played in most types of weather, but only the truly proficient golfer can find an excuse in any season. My goal with this chapter is to help you recognize that every round of golf is played in environmental conditions, the elements of which can adversely affect your performance. Being able to turn a sliced tee shot into a weather related excuse even in "perfect conditions" separates the novice excuse-maker from the one you can become.

*A.   Too Cold*

I remember one December I was home from college during break when I got a call from my friend Steve. "I called Tamarack and they are open. Let's go." I told him to pick me up in 20 minutes. Now we did not live in Florida or Arizona. We were not in Georgia or Texas. Nope, we lived in New Jersey, and there was snow on the ground. A lesser person might have thought golfing in such weather was insane. We saw an opportunity. The course would be wide open. And, in the event we did not play great, well there was snow on the ground and it was 19 degrees, what could you expect. The point was that we were not about to give up a round of golf, especially when the excuse was built in.

I vividly recall stepping up to the first tee. A relatively short par-4 with a lake on the right side. The fairway was shaped like a "C" so that you had to play your tee shot left to avoid the water and then your approach to the green needed to avoid the water as well. Clad in snow pants, a ski jacket, winter gloves (with a golf glove underneath for when it was my shot) and a hat, I prepared to hit my first shot. I took off my winter gloves, gripped my driver and let 'er rip. The ball started slicing almost immediately and head directly for the water. "Dammit!" Then, a miracle. The pond had frozen over. My ball hit the water and bounced all the way across onto the green...just like I drew it up on the tee.

Now clearly, mammoth drive aside, this was not one of the better rounds of golf I have ever played. As any supportive parent would have, mine told me that I was a moron, could not have expected to play a decent round and of course deserved the head cold I got the next day. But for me it did not matter because how often do you get to play a round of golf with such a perfect and undeniable excuse: it was freezing and there was snow on the ground.

There does not need to be snow on the ground for you to use the cold as an excuse. Remember, no one knows how you feel. What is cold to one person might be warm to another. If there is even a remotely plausible semi-believable chance that it could potentially be considered less than perfectly warm, then you can blame the cold.

Close your eyes and picture the following situation. You are standing in the center of the fairway after a perfect drive on a 443 yard par 4. You have 195 yards to the center of a large green that is protected by bunkers left and right. There is a small stream about 15 feet wide that cuts through the fairway starting 70 yards in front of you. The sun ducks behind the clouds again, making it even colder than it already is on this chilly September afternoon. When you teed off the temperature was a comfortable 60 degrees, but since then has dipped into the high-50's. All round your long irons have been crisp and on target and you are supremely confident that another solid iron shot is about to occur. You start your takeaway. It is flawless. You transition nicely. The downswing feels perfect. At contact your steel shaft vibrates in your hands sending pain shooting through your wrists. It is as if someone switched out your balata ball with a hunk of iron. The ball, predictably goes 6 inches off the ground for 70 yards directly into the water. Congratulations, you are now hitting your fourth shot. Sound familiar?

As you attempt to get feeling back in your hands your playing partner tells you it looks like you picked your head up at contact. A novice excuse artist might thank him for the tip, or acknowledge the fact with a simple nod in agreement. But not you. You quickly correct your colleague, "Not at all. It is just so cold out here that I could not get a good grip on the club. My swing is fine."

Some cynics might retort that you decided to play in the cold weather, so you should suffer the consequences. These people must be rebuffed with prejudice. You are not god. You do not control the weather. You are simply trying to take advantage of one of the last opportunities you have to golf this season. The key to remember, it is not your fault, it was the cold weather that ruined your shot.

*B. Too Hot*

Cold weather and reverberating irons are not the only weather related excuses that exist. Just as it can be too cold to play, it can also be too hot. Heat, especially extreme heat, can play tricks on your mind and drain your body of energy. In such situations, it is vitally important that you stay mentally sharp so that any miscue can be rationally blamed on the true cause, the heat.

Most of us have played a round of golf when our hands were sweaty causing an imperfect grip or perspiration to drip into our eyes causing a momentary loss of focus. In these cases, one must always remember that trees offer shade! Thus, any shot into the woods is not a mishit, but rather a calculated decision designed to get out of the sun and preserve valuable electrolytes for later in the round.

For example, imagine you are playing a 540-yard par 5. The thermometer has not dipped below 90-degrees all day long. The plastic on your cart is nearly melting from the sweltering heat. You survey the hole. There is not a lot of danger other than the water running down the right side starting about 200-yards from the tee box. Your tee shot travels 270 yards into the first cut of the rough on the left side (hey, not all of our shots can find the fairway). As you prepare for your second shot, you use your towel to wipe beads of sweat off of your head, arms and hands. If only you could cool off somehow. You take your stance, begin your swing and, being completely sapped of your energy, hit your shot directly into the water hazard. Before you take your drop, wet your towel with the water from the hazard, wipe down your head and arms. Now that you have cooled off and feel rejuvenated, you stick your approach to 3-feet and make the putt. "Nice par" your buddy tells you, "too bad you hit it in the water, it could have been a birdie."

This is when the mental part of the game becomes essential. You were only lying one in the rough and your second shot went into the water but traveled 150 yards. Thus, for your fourth shot, you only had 120 yards into the green. Even if you did not stick it close, a decent approach would have afforded you the chance to save bogey, or maybe even make par with a long putt. So, instead of thanking your friend, how should you respond? Easy. "Too bad? Why do you say that? You think I did that by accident? Dude, it is nearly 100-degrees out here and I am melting. I could barely cool off. I needed to wet my towel so I could cool myself down. I knew how far I needed to hit my second so that it both went into the water and left me a comfortable distance to stick my wedge." Then turn and walk away as if there is nothing else to discuss.

Any doctor will tell you that protecting your skin from the harmful elements is vitally important. Truthfully, you should wear sunscreen every time you play and the sun is out because prolonged exposure can damage your skin. Unfortunately, sun tan lotion can be greasy and can burn if it gets into your eyes. When you are playing and the sun is shining, never forget the protection sun tan lotion provides to your skin *and your game*. When you have a poor hole, remind your playing partner of the weather subtly. When you head to the next tee, a simple "Now that I've wiped the sun tan lotion off of my hands hopefully I will have a better grip on my clubs this hole." A nonverbal hint will also suffice in this scenario. Before driving to the next hole, make sure to dramatically pour water onto your golf towel and then dab your eyes (adding, "Ah, that's better" helps). When your partner asks you what you are doing, he has in actuality set you up perfectly: "On my approach, some suntan lotion dripped into my eyes and started to burn. I could hardly see on any of those three putts."

One last point with respect to the hot weather. We, as humans, must never be selfish on a golf course. At its core, golf is a game of dignity and respect for all things. And, just as you can get hot, so can your ball. Any shot into the water should not be viewed as a swing mistake, but rather as allowing your ball to escape the heat. Do not ever let your playing partners blame the breakdown of your follow through for a tailing slice in 90-degree weather that happens to land in the middle of a lake. No, instead point out your spiritual side that is finely in tune with all objects. Your sensitive nature understood that the ball was hot and needed relief. For bonus points, make sure to point out your playing partner's utter lack of compassion and look at her with a frown and disdain.

*C. Too Windy*

"Come on! Get there! Son of a..." If these screams of an exasperated golfer sound at all familiar to you, then you have likely played golf in the wind. Windy conditions elicit some of the easiest and most common excuses from golfers. Unfortunately, most golfers use the same excuse over and over again, "The wind took it." At some point, saying this too much just makes you look inept. After all, if the wind took your last 15 shots and blew them 20 yards to the right, then maybe you should learn and aim farther left. Similarly, if there has been a steady 2-club wind all round and you continue to come up short on your approach shots, whose fault is that?

The key for wind-related excuses is creativity. Remember, the worst thing that can happen is that your playing partner does not believe your lie and then you never play with him or her again. To illustrate this point, I am reminded of a round of golf I played on The Champion course at PGA National Resort & Spa, host of the Honda Classic. The Champion boasts a three-hole stretch known as "The Bear Trap." For most amateur golfers it might as well be called the Seventh Circle of Hell.

The first of hole of The Bear Trap is the 179 yard par-3 over water to a narrow green that angles from front left to back right, has a bunker and a huge hill on the left side. For reasons known only to the golf gods, this hole plays into a fierce wind 99 times out of 100. Going into the hole with a one-stroke lead, Raymond Floyd famously made a quadruple-bogey 7 during the final round of the 1994 Senior Championship. Needless to say, it is not an easy hole.

While visiting my parents one year, my father, his friend and I, decided to play The Champion. Conservatively, I would estimate that the wind was blowing 400 miles per hour that day, though my father thinks it was closer to 35 miles per hour. Having not played in several months, and this being just my third round of the trip, I had already utilized to perfection my excuses from Chapter 2. Coming off of an unsatisfying double-bogey, I was determined to handle The Bear Trap. I envisioned my Bogey-Birdie-Par trip through the trap from the prior year and was confident I could once again play these three holes well. The tees were up slightly so we had 165 yards to the pin. Playing ready golf, I stepped to the tee, 4-iron in hand. I generally hit my 4-iron 200 yards, so I was sure I had enough club. Standing over the ball, my hat blew right off my head. I made a mental note to store that as a possible excuse for when my ball failed to find the bottom of the cup off the tee. I stepped off, put my hat back on and rebuffed my caddie's suggestion that I move up to a 5-wood. I was young and brash, and after I hit my tee shot I was laying three.

I pured it, right on the sweet spot. It looked good for a few seconds, heading straight for the pin. Immediately, this thought went through my head: "Remember, when you miss your hole-in-one by a foot, your hat blew off." Alas, it just could not fight its way through the wind and dropped into the water. When I turned around my father, as only a loving and supportive father can, said "Maybe next time you listen to your caddie, dummy." Little did he know that standing on the tee box I was able to feel something he could not, and it was my duty to inform him of that: "No. The wind kicked up. You guys are under the trees and cannot feel it. But from up here I could feel the wind increase. I hit it great, had it not been for that extra gust I'd be 15 feet. Let's see what you can do tough guy." As a side note, my father and I have a great relationship premised on true values, such as love, patience and of course, talking trash.

So my elderly, decrepit, 24-handicapper father (see, trash talk) stepped to the tee. "Take your driver old man." He turned and smirked, clearly he thought this was his chance. His time to shine. He would hit it close and then mock me mercilessly. Then he proceeded to hit his 3-wood into the water. Without missing a beat he turned to the rest of us, "See what a good father I am. I felt bad for my son, so I decided to join him for some father-son bonding." Not as believable as my real excuse, but he got an A for effort. Still, there were two more golfers to go.

Third to the tee was a gentleman who had the misfortune of being grouped with my father, his friend and me. Immediately upon shanking his drive on the first hole, he utilized the old classic, "I just had a lesson and was trying something" (see Chapter 8.D). Apparently he had been "trying something" all round because I think he had one par and 13 triples. At any rate, Mr. Trying-Something stepped to the tee, hit a good shot but also suffered the wrath of the wind at The Bear Trap. Expecting another "I just had a lesson" excuse, we were all pleasantly surprised by his creative excuse: "I was so moved by your father's display of compassion for you that I felt I should display the same compassion for him."

Finally Jeff, my father's friend, stepped to the tee. So far, three up and three in. Before he hit, we offered him the chance to save his ball from drowning and simply join us at the drop area. Quite naturally he refused and any experienced golfer can tell you what happened next. Yep, his ball went about 50 yards to the left of the green, left of the water, left of the trap and left of the mounds guarding the trap that guarded the green. "Well, I saw you three morons go in the water, so I figured I needed to aim a little more left."

My father, Jeff and Mr. Trying-Something each exhibited a fundamental component for any golf excuse: creativity. Unable to adapt their swing to the wind, they instead drew upon my "real" excuse of the wind kicking up. Obviously two of these excuses are weak. Anyone who met my father knows very well that he would rather rub in a good shot after your poor shot, than hit a poor shot to commiserate. And, as for Mr. Trying-Something, he probably should have stuck with the "I just had a lesson" approach; after all, consistency is important in golf. Jeff's excuse on the other hand is at least plausible in that many amateur golfers tend to overcompensate based on a deficient shot by a playing partner. So we will let that one slide by and not point out that he was way too quick with his swing.

The point of the anecdote above is that falling back on the same old tired excuse "The wind took it" is not acceptable. In windy conditions, there are many excuses available to you. Even if your playing partners do not believe you farther than you can top a driver, they will appreciate the effort you put forth.

*D. Too Dry*

I have to admit that when I first heard someone complain about the course being too dry I was slightly taken aback. It was not so much the excuse, as it was the timing of the excuse. He had not failed to hold a green or ran a putt 10 feet by the hole; rather, he duck hooked his tee shot through the rough and a small line of trees separating the adjacent fairway. His ball then proceeded to run through the other fairway into the rough on the right side of that hole. When he turned to me, exasperated, and said that his ball did not deserve to be in the rough I was clearly perplexed. With complete conviction, he explained to me that the course was too dry and on a better maintained course his ball would have come to rest in the fairway, albeit the adjacent fairway. The logic of his argument was hard to dispute.

I would like to tell you that he recovered nicely and scrambled to save par, or even bogey. But alas, that was not the case. Following his quadruple bogey (and several off-color remarks about the dried out condition of the ADJACENT fairway) he told me that such a catastrophe would never happen on any other course he plays. My response, while somewhat cruel, was to be expected: "How many times do you duck hook your tee shot into an opposing fairway?" Not deterred, he proceeded to complain to each of the next two rangers we saw and even had the gall to go into the pro-shop after the round and lodge a formal complaint.

Two lessons should be taken from this anecdote. First, and this cannot be overstated, COMMIT TO YOUR EXCUSE. No matter how ridiculous he sounded making his complaints, and I have to believe deep down somewhere inside he knew he was defying logic, he stayed the course. Second, creativity is essential. Never be afraid to blame the first thing that comes into your mind, even if it is the condition of an adjacent hole.

The preceding story notwithstanding, there are certainly times when a dried out course can wreak havoc on your game. The beautiful thing about these times is that any golfer worth his salt will concur, thus reserving the same excuse for themselves later in the round or, if the excuse is not needed, being able to boast regarding his skill level in conquering such difficult conditions.

One word of warning that you must consider. As with other weather-related excuses, do not use them too often in one round. If you race your putts 10 feet past the hole for 18 consecutive holes and blame the dry greens, your fellow golfers will probably think the heat melted your brain because you cannot adapt to the conditions. Similarly, if you find that the greens are so hard that you keep running your approach shots off the back, try going down one club. Sometimes it is actually better to play good golf then give a good excuse for poor golf. And, if you find yourself in dire straits searching for another excuse, well that is why I wrote this book. Keep it in your golf bag and refer to it when no one else is looking…just do not get caught otherwise you will need an excuse for why you are reading a book on the course, and that is a different book.

*E. Too Rainy*

Everyone has played in a misty haze, and most people have even played in a slight drizzle. But only the true golf fanatic—or as my father would call them, idiots—will play through a steady driving rain. The excuses that follow below can be used in any wet-weather scenario, but only you can be the judge of whether the weather will undermine or further your excuse.

One of my very close friends got married in Jacksonville, Florida. The day after the wedding, his new father-in-law took me and one other guy golfing at TPC Sawgrass, one of my favorite golf courses ever. For weeks leading up to that weekend, I had played Tiger Woods Golf on my Playstation, learning the ins and outs of each hole, where to hit my approach shots and how the greens broke. Sure, it is not the ideal practice round, but we amateurs do not have the luxury of playing a practice round the day before the real round like professional golfers. Round after round I shot in the low 60's or high 50's. When the time came to play the real course, I was ready.

One crucial error I made in all those practice rounds was that I never played in poor conditions (that, and I used the golfer I created who was essentially a golf god). For days leading up to the wedding, the weather report was not optimistic so I ended up not bringing my clubs (we will revisit this round and excuse in Chapter 9.C). Finally the day arrived. It was overcast and the rain was coming at some point, but we ventured out anyway. After all, how many times do you get to play one of the greatest public courses in the country?

Drizzle and mist dominated the front nine, and the skies finally opened up on the 11th tee. It was officially a downpour. But, no lightening, so we continued. On the tee of the short par-4 12th hole things quickly lost control, literally. It was raining so hard that I decided I absolutely wanted no part of the rough, so I would tee off with a 5-iron and (hopefully) put it right down the middle of the fairway. On my take away my hands slipped up the shaft of the club ever so slightly. I knew something was wrong immediately upon my club making contact.

Now, I am not sure exactly how much of the 12th tee I decided to move with that shot, but suffice it to say that it looked like I was helping them demolish the tee box entirely. The club had slipped in my hand just enough so that about three inches before reaching my ball, the head of my club dug deep into the ground and sent the dirt flying off the front of the tee box. Not only did the dirt go flying, but my club followed, landing about 15 feet in front of the tee box. In fact, the only thing that did not make it off the tee box was the ball.

A lesser man might have blamed the rain. Another might have blamed the wet ground behind the ball. I chose a different path. I looked at my friend's new father-in-law and said: "I knew I should have hit the 5-wood. No way would it have dug into the ground like that."

Needless to say that was enough to convince my playing partners that perhaps we had come to the end of our round. We picked our balls up, drove to my 5-iron, and decided to call it a day. But, instead of going directly to the clubhouse, we decided to drive the course so I could get a look at what I was missing. By the time we made it to the 14th tee the rain had stopped and the sun came out (you have to love Florida weather). We put down bogey-bogey for 12 and 13 and continued on our merry way.

The comment about changing from 5-wood to 5-iron was just one of the many, many plausible excuses (at least plausible to me) that one can rely upon in the rain. The tried and true "the club slipped in my hand" is always an easy fallback. However, the point of this book is not to just give the easy excuses, but to help you expand your repertoire.

Let us think about what else can go wrong. A wet ball can pick up dirt, sand, mud or even a blade of grass causing it to roll off line on a putt, even a 4-inch gimmie that you should have just picked up instead of trying to be a hero (remember, even the pros take gimmies when offered during match-play). One misstep and you could be ankle deep in a puddle causing that side of your body to become colder and heavier thus throwing off your equilibrium for the remainder of the round. If you are at a course that does not have covered golf carts, your butt could get soaked from sitting on water. Sure, this could be avoided by wiping down your seat with a towel, but voluntarily throwing away a classic excuse such as "My butt is wet and uncomfortable" would be pure madness. In really wet weather, your club could go flying out of your hand, but it is tough to use that as an excuse if you are still holding onto your club, so use this one sparingly.

There are many more excuses to be had based on the rain, so I encourage you to keep your eyes open for them, just do not let the rain get into your eyes, it could affect your vision on any shot. So, with these building blocks for rain-based excuses, we will move on after this one last thought: in the immortal words of Milli Vanilli, or rather the people who were actually singing for them, "Blame it on the Rain."

*F. Too Humid*

Humidity is frustrating to deal with in any situation. Nothing is worse than walking out of your house, car or apartment and immediately feeling like you need a shower after you just took one. Personally, I would rather play in the rain than in high humidity; maybe that is why my dad always tells me I am an idiot. Nonetheless, humidity does offer various excuses that we can all use without fear of reprisal. Let me explain.

When it is humid, our clothes stick to us, our body parts stick to other body parts and we just never feel comfortable. These are the undeniable side effects of humidity. If you are unfortunate enough to be golfing in humid weather, why not take advantage of the immutable laws of humidity.

If your underwear starts riding up on you during a business meeting, obviously the appropriate approach is to wiggle in your chair until it becomes dislodged and hope that no one noticed. In golf, however, feel free to share this information with any one of your group. Sliced a tee shot? "My underwear was riding up." Missed a two foot putt for bogey? "My tee shirt was stuck to my arms." Bunker shot did not get out of the bunker? "I hate this freaking weather, I am so miserable I just want to whack someone over the head with my sand wedge." I guarantee no one in your group will call you out after that excuse. Try not to use this one with complete strangers as it may make for some uncomfortable times during the rest of the round.

Humidity may be one of the more frustrating weather conditions in which to play, but that should not stop you from using it to your advantage. Never let the weather get the best of your excuse-making abilities. If you do, you might just have to become a better golfer and frankly who has the time or money for that kind of time commitment.

G. *Too Many Animals Around*

i. For those of you that actually bought this book and are not related to my family, thank you. And, since you do not know me, let me take this opportunity to tell you that I grew up in New Jersey and now live in New York City. Consequently, I tend to play all of my golf in either New Jersey or New York – I know, shocking. Well, for those of you not from this neck of the woods, let me tell you a couple of things. First, New York City is the greatest city on the planet; you can get pizza, toothpaste or even duct tape at 4 A.M. (sure, only one of those things makes any sense, but the point still stands). Second, other than Exit 13 off of the New Jersey Turnpike, New Jersey does not smell as bad as everyone says. And finally, if you play golf up here, you must allow for the bug-factor, and it just gets worse the closer you get to "The Shore" (for those of you non-Jerseyites, that is what we call the beach).

Golfing in the Tri-State Area can pose several different obstacles, but no obstacle looms larger than the mosquito.[1] These bloodsucking little creatures love golf courses, especially, it seems, when I am playing.

I recall one time at a course that should have been name Mosquito Valley, I was standing on the tee box and got bitten simultaneously by two different mosquitoes even though I had thoroughly doused myself in bug spray. As a quick aside, insect

---

[1] Mosquitoes are common flying insects in the family Culicidae that are found around the world. There are about 3,500 species. See, I am not here just to teach about golf, but also about science because I am a helper, it's what I do. And kids, this counts are you science lesson for the day, so go watch some TV now.

repellant has my vote for the biggest rip-off known to man, it might as well be insect attractant for as well as it works. Anyway, I digress. So I am standing on the tee box preparing to smoke a drive straight down the middle of the fairway on a short par-4 when, just as I finish my backswing, two mosquitoes bite me: one on the head, the other the leg. My ball careened into the woods hit about 400 trees and settled down nicely in between the roots of a huge tree. My only option was to hack, duck and pray. Thankfully, I escaped without injury, well physical injury anyway. After I tapped in for double-par I swore to all things holy that it would be my life-long mission to kill all the mosquitoes. The guys I was playing just laughed…until the mosquitoes got them: then we were a team, joining forces against the mosquitoes that we have renamed bogey-monsters (not to be confused with the boogy-monster that lived in my closet growing up).

Mosquitoes do not only ruin individual shots, they have been known to take down entire rounds of golf. I was golfing with my father one time and he actually left the course after 11 holes. He had just had enough. When I arrived home after the round I found him talking to his friend on the phone extolling the virtues of his swing that lead him to shoot a 78. Now, being the loving and respectful son that I am, I immediately picked up the phone and without wasting time to find out who he was talking to, I let the ear on the other end of the phone know that he had in fact shot a 78, but it was after 11 holes and he was a big baby and left because the itty-witty buggies beat up the big bad human.

The moral of these mosquito-related stories is of great import, so take note: mosquitoes, like most other insects can be extremely annoying and since they are so small no one can question you that one bit you during a swing. If it is not a particularly buggy day (or if you happen to be playing golf indoors on a golf simulator) and want to use this excuse, it is very easy to sell by smacking your leg/arm/neck and screaming out "Damn, he got me!"

   ii. Mosquitoes are not the only creatures that have had adverse affects on either mine or my playing partner's game. Two stories, one funny and one scary come to mind. Which do you want to hear first? Oh, right, you are reading this so you have no choice. We will start with the scary one first.

Playing golf in Arizona offers the opportunity to play on some of the most magnificent course settings with the beautiful bright green of the golf course set against the desert sands and cradled in the mountains that change colors as the sun moves across the sky. Of course, playing in Arizona also offers the opportunity to die. Let me clarify. During law school, I organized a golf trip to Scottsdale, Arizona for a few buddies. Having arrived a day earlier than my friends I decided to play a couple of rounds on my own. On the first tee of my first round, I promptly sliced a ball into the desert sand, not more than 10 yards from where the rough meets the sand. This being my first ever time golfing in Arizona and thus not being familiar with Arizona golf, I started to walk to my ball. That's when I heard the screams of the two gentlemen with whom I was paired. "Don't go in there!" they exclaimed. "Why not?" They answered with one simple word, "Rattlers." They proceeded to inform me that when the rattlesnakes are out, it is local rule (or at least their local rule) not to go into the desert to find or hit your ball, just take a free drop in the rough and pray your errant shot didn't upset a rattlesnake that knew you were hitting a Titleist. For the rest of that round and the succeeding few days, and remember I learned this lesson on the first hole of my first round, I instituted the rattlesnake excuse: "I thought I heard a rattle". It was simple and believable, which are the two keys to any good excuse. Okay, so maybe that wasn't exactly a "scary" story, but if you heard those guys yelling at you when you were about to step into a snake-infested desert, I bet you would have been at least a little scared…or am I just a big baby?

The funny story still makes my friend Brett and me crack-up every time that we retell it. We were playing this municipal course down by the Jersey shore called Ocean County at Atlantis. At the turn, we stopped at the food shack so Brett could get a hot dog. A little mustard, a little relish and we were off to the 10th tee. By way of background, Atlantis is a heavily wooded golf course and the 10th hole was no different; the tee box was surrounded on three sides by tall trees. I hit my tee shot and then Brett placed his hot dog on the golf cart seat and got ready to hit his drive while I stood quietly on the tee box behind him. Just as he was getting ready to swing, I saw something out of the corner of my eye: a squirrel had jumped into our cart and was eating Brett's hotdog. I started laughing hysterically, so Brett turned to see what was going on. Now, Brett is a big guy and does not like to share his food with his wife or daughter, so you can imagine that he was none too thrilled to see a little squirrel eating his lunch. He ran after that squirrel with driver in hand and the squirrel took off with hot dog in mouth. I dropped to the ground laughing. For the next 9 holes every time either one of us hit a bad a shot we would say the following, "I just keep thinking of that damn squirrel with that hot dog in his mouth."[2]

Now, I will grant you that this excuse is a little unique and peculiar to this one scenario, but the point remains: animals can provide the basis for some of the best excuses.

*H. Unable to See*

---

[2] Have no fear, we returned to the food shack and got Brett another hot dog…on the house.

As I mentioned previously, I love playing golf early in the morning. The earlier the better. Early morning golf allows me to play quickly, play before it gets too hot and most importantly, get home to my wife before she wakes up so that I do not get any grief about spending my day golfing instead of with her. Not that she would give me any such grief because she knows better—just kidding (I love you honey, please don't make me sleep on the couch when you read this).

One of the drawbacks of teeing off before the sun rises is that the sun is not up yet, which makes seeing a little difficult (while I like to play early in the morning, these excuses are just as applicable at dusk). For the skeptics amongst you who think it is important to see while you are golfing, I have only name for you: Pat W. Browne Jr. Pat is a blind golf champion who once defeated Payne Stewart by 20 strokes in a 9-hole golf match in which Payne played blindfolded.

Of course, if this were a book about overcoming obstacles I would delve deeper into Mr. Browne's life and story. But alas, it is not, it is a book about *stretching the truth* and making up excuses. Thus, early morning golf provides the solid, "Well I couldn't see where I was aiming" excuse. Many times during early morning golf you will run into someone who does not believe in using excuses. These holier than thou types will often attempt to debunk your excuse with a surly comment along the lines of "Just aim down the middle and swing." HA! If you could just aim down the middle, make your swing and have your ball end up where you were aiming, you would have never purchased this book (unless you are a relative of mine or a friend of my mother's).

No, no, no. When it is dark out, you have hundreds of excuses at your disposal. One caveat, though, is that you have to use them *when it is actually dark out*. If you start telling people you cannot see where you are aiming and it is 11:30 AM, they will most likely tell you to open your eyes or take your head out of your butt.

Without the sun you have a decreased sense of depth-perception. Without that giant warming ball of magma in the sky you cannot properly decipher the break on your 6-foot birdie putt. You are also unable to see the bunker/water trap/tree/person that your ball landed in or hit. I even played with someone who once told me that it was so dark out that he nearly drove off the cart path (into the rough mind you) and was so shaken that the double-bogey 7 he just made should really have been a par so he would split the difference on his scorecard.

There is one other excuse that always comes in handy during the wee hours of the morning or around dusk. I frequently hear, "Well I couldn't see where it ended up, but it was going 275 down the middle, so even though I cannot find it, this is where it should be" right before I hear these words "I am dropping it here and not taking a penalty stroke, it is not my fault it is dark out." Personally, I have never been a big fan of blaming God for the whole darkness-thing and not taking a penalty stroke, but feel free to use that excuse if you fear no wrath in the afterlife. Other than eternal damnation, the one other pitfall with this is excuse is that if you do not drive it 275 down the middle several times when it is light out, everyone will know you are a big liar. To avoid this problem, tell your group it was only going 250 yards, that is a much easier distance to accomplish.

Problems seeing can be caused by factors other than just the lack of the sun's presence. In 2003, my friend Brett and I decided to take a drive up to The Concord Resort & Spa in Kiamesha Lake, New York to play the Monster Course (roughly 15 thousand yards from the tips, though I could be slightly off on that figure). We had the first tee time of the day because we decided we would play 36-holes. There was only one tiny problem with our rationale. When we wanted to tee off, the course was covered in a blanket of fog. We literally could not see our golf cart from the tee box. After waiting about 20-30 minutes, the starter told us we would just have to play through the fog. He said "Don't worry, just hit it straight and you'll probably find it."

"That's great," Brett said, "but what happens when we are in the fairway and the group behind us tees off because they can't see us?" The starter's response: "Play fast." Not wanting to hold everyone else up, we agreed that we would hit our tee shots and if we could not find our balls we would take a penalty stroke but drop in the fairway at our average drive distance. Miraculously, we found both our balls (mine was in the fairway, thank you very much). Of course, not wanting to get plunked on the head, we both rushed our approach shots and ended up making a disaster out of the first hole. On the green, we agreed that we both would have scored much better but we were worried about getting hit. This was a classic example of two players agreeing to believe each other's lie since they were exactly the same.

The fog burned off by the time we reached the second tee, but thankfully it had rained a lot that week and the course was pretty wet so I had a lot of other excuses at my disposal.

4.     IT'S NOT YOUR SWING, IT'S YOUR EQUIPMENT

Nothing makes a golfer more excited then buying a new club, or better yet a set of clubs. Year after year, golf equipment manufacturers introduce newer, better technology to allow even the worst golfer to hit the ball longer, straighter or with better spin. Of course, just because the technology improved, does not mean your swing improved. In fact, that is why one of the biggest marketing techniques of manufacturers is telling customers that these new clubs are more forgiving on mis-hits. Translation, "we know you are not a very good golfer, but if you just put a close to decent swing on the ball, this club will help turn that triple bogey into a double."

One thing new technology can never obviate, however, is the need for excuses, and in fact new clubs often serve as one of the most popular excuses heard on a course. This chapter not only deals with excuses for new clubs, but also discusses other equipment-related excuses, such as: the putter; old clubs; rental clubs; missing a club; shoes; and bad balls.

A.     *New Clubs*

We have all done it before, and it is a near certainty that we will all do it again. We see a commercial or print ad for the "next great club" and we decide that our old clubs no longer suit our game. So a few hundred, or maybe thousand, dollars later we are ready to take on Tiger with our new arsenal of clubs.

I remember sitting on the couch one evening with my parents when a commercial came on for the Orlimar Trimetal. It supposedly made it impossible to not get your tee shot in the air because of lower-weighting, a new composite material on the club face and I think it even had turbo-chargers. Having just graduated college, my uncle told me he was going to buy me a driver since I did not have one at the time. This was it; this was the club that was going to help me finally break into the 80's. It had to be. After all, the swing machine hit it solid every time and the mis-hits went farther than those of the other clubs they tested. So, like any other sucker for golf innovations, I called and ordered my Trimetal (the money-back guarantee made my decision that much easier).

I remember that the day that club came I headed out to the course, ready to shot an 82 or 83. The first hole on the West Course at Tamarack County Course, the course I grew up playing, is a relatively short par-4 that bends slightly from right to left. Would I hit it 270 down the middle with a little draw or maybe it would go 300? I stepped to the tee with baited breath.

Even with the confidence I had with this new club, I made sure to tell the guy I was playing with about my new purchase, you know, just in case. That first tee shot nearly killed a host of worms and ants in front of the tee box. The ball never got more then 3 feet off the ground, falling well short of the fairway. I turned to my playing partner and instinctively told him that I was not used to the weighting of the club because of the special materials used in the clubface.

Two holes later I had another chance. Thank god the third hole was a short par-5, because apparently I still was not used to the weighting of the clubface. In fact, after several rounds, and an awfully large number of topped tee shots later, I determined that the weighting and not anything else (read: my swing) was the issue. Everyone I played with for those few rounds was told that it was my first round with this new club—the beauty of playing with strangers—and I just needed to get used to it. The truth was that I needed to order something new, so the Trimetal made its long journey back to the manufacturer. As an aside, I was fortunate to find the perfect driver for me a few weeks after I started taking lessons, what a coincidence.

Just like a new driver, new irons take an adjustment as well. During this adjustment phase, it is critical that you have mastery of the appropriate "new club" excuses. A couple of years ago I switched from King Cobra II irons to the Nike Slingshot OSS (we will get to the reason for the switch in the next section). Strangely enough, these clubs were also weighted differently.

However, I had hit them on the range several times and I knew they were definitely the club I preferred. So I made the purchase. For the first five rounds I informed everyone I played with on the first tee that "I just bought new clubs and am getting used to them, so I can't make any promises." I find it is always better to set other's expectations low so that when you perform well you can really rub it in their face.

After I got used to the weighting, because that excuse can only last so long before you have to either return your clubs or admit you might not be the best golfer ever, I had to address another issue. I remember one round with my father I hit my 8-iron from 155 yards out and came up about 10 yards short and right. Before I could even say anything, he cut me off, "There's no wind ma'am, so what's your excuse." "Frankly," I told him, "I am shocked at your ignorance. I just bought new clubs and the distances on these are different so I have to get those straight." And just like the supportive and loving father he is, he responded, "Okay, but you still went right, did the club do that also?" The lesson here, some shots require multiple excuses, so never lose focus.

The weighting and distance issues are not the only excuses to be utilized during those first few, or thirty, rounds with new clubs. One of my greatest inspirations for this chapter is my mother, who has purchased more new clubs than any person I have ever met. She has provided me with many "new club excuses" over the years, and with her blessing, please feel free to use one or more of the following excuses: (1) politely inform your group that the sweet spot on your new clubs is in a slightly different location and you are still in the process of working out your new swing mechanics; (2) new clubs mean new grips, and new grips pose a plethora of problems, such as being too thick or to thin so your hands are not comfortable. New grips could be too sticky or too slippery, so your hold on the club is not as secure or comfortable as usual; and (3) new clubs look different, so visually you might have to take time adjusting to the view from your set-up.

Beyond physical components of new clubs, there are other issues that could arise. When you are certain your ball did not go into the rough where everyone else in your group thought it did, or if you simply stopped tracking your ball but do not want to get caught for that error, you should be aware that your ability to track your new ball flight can be affected because of the launch trajectory on new clubs. The point is that new clubs offer new excuses, so be sure to keep your eyes open for any that might crop up; then use those excuses for as long as they are believable.

B.  *Old Clubs*

So why did I buy new clubs? Well, I was sure my clubs were broken. Every time that I hit a ball it sounded like a baseball bat hitting a golf ball. Time after time, I was hearing this sound. I was convinced, and made it known to everyone I played with, that I must have worn out the sweet spot on these clubs. Old clubs means old technology. And, while new clubs have their own issues that you have to deal with, chances are that you will not be playing with both old and new clubs at one time so you do not have to worry about inapposite excuses.

Old clubs contain the physical manifestations of years of wear and tear. Professionals replace their clubs often because of worn out grooves that prevent the ability to achieve the proper spin. Of course, professionals do not have to pay for these new clubs. All professionals have to do is call Nike, Ping, Titleist or whatever other manufacturer they use and say "Hey, give me clubs" and presto, new clubs appear. For the rest of us normal people, replacing new clubs every season is cost-prohibitive, whereas purchasing this book most certainly was not. So, rather than purchasing new clubs, the common person can simply rely on this chapter to "explain" the cause for his or her poor play.

No matter how old your clubs are they share one common thread with all other old clubs: they are not new. While you may not see the genius of this statement initially, you must acknowledge that it is true. The beauty of this statement is its simplicity.

Since old clubs are not new, they do not possess the newest and best technology. As a consequence, you are playing with substandard equipment. This is especially useful if you are playing with someone who has newer clubs than you. If you hit a tee shot with your two year old driver and the shot goes 200 yards forward and 100 yards to the right, are you to blame? Of course not. As you walk off the tee box, the simple comment, "Hey, that's about the best I can do with substandard equipment" should do the trick. If your playing partner is using equally substandard equipment, chances are he or she will not refute such a statement but rather store it for his or her next poor tee shot.

And, if your playing partner has newer equipment, add this gem, "I'm not made of money. We can't *all* afford the latest and greatest equipment." Your partner will feel so guilty about his indulgent spending practices that there is no way he will call you out on your excuse. Well, unless he is a relative, really good friend or heartless soul (his lack of emotional support could also be a reason for your lack of focus).

Controlling one's emotions is essential during a round of golf. But, even the pros have trouble containing themselves all of the time. During The Masters in 2008, Brandt Snedeker was playing the 13th hole when he put his lay-up into Rae's Creek for the second straight day. Clearly frustrated, the camera caught

Brandt bending his club, and for a second I thought he might snap it in half. In true professional form, however, Brandt controlled himself and handed the club back to his caddie.

Many of us amateurs are not as composed. How many times have you slammed your club into the ground following a poor shot? Even more benignly, how many times has your takeaway or follow through hit a tree, rock or some other inanimate object? Each time your club makes contact with such an item it takes a toll on your club. This consequence is actually a famous law of physics: Newton's Third Law, the law of reciprocal actions. As with any good scientific experiment, let us analyze the procedure for implementing a scientific law excuse.

The next time you are playing with old clubs and hit a poor shot, make sure your partner knows that this club has been through the wars and may be slightly bent at the hozzle or has a dented clubface that clearly negatively influenced your shot. When your colleague gives you a look of disdain or distrust, or even worse, rejects your excuse, be prepared. In a condescending tone ask: "Have you never heard of Newton's Third Law, the law of reciprocal actions?" Most likely your opponent will be flummoxed. Calmly explain to him that you have had these clubs for nearly a decade and in that time, through no fault of your own, they have become slightly worn and are no longer in pristine condition because every time you hit a tree, the tree hit back. Yes, as Newton's Third Law explains, "For every action there is an equal and opposite reaction." When your club hit a tree, the tree also hit your club causing an ever so slight alignment issue. Normally, your proficiency allows you to overcome such an issue, but the laws of physics are undeniable. If nothing else, this should provide enough frustration in your opponent's game to cause some mistakes. When that happens, explain that those errors are likely the result of physics as well. Then watch as he quickly adopts your rationale.

Old clubs also require maintenance and whether you have this maintenance performed or not, there are excuses to be had. Grips get worn down and shafts need to be replaced. If you have not had either, or both, of these physical problems rectified then they are sure to cause shanks, slices, duffs and muffs. If you have had these issues fixed, then errant shots are likely due to the adjustment period associated with such repairs.

One issue that cannot be solved by sending your club to the shop is the dulling of grooves. Worn out grooves affect your touch and ability to impart spin or stop the ball on the green. Even if you never had the skill to accomplish these goals in the first place, your playing partner does not know that, but what he does know (after you show him) is that the reason your ball went flying 40 feet past the hole was because the grooves on your old clubs are worn down.

One last point on old clubs. If you rely on this excuse throughout a round, or over the course of several rounds, you might be faced with a player that questions your refusal to replace the clubs. If the money excuse outlined above will not work, get ready to act. Somberly look at him and point out that these clubs belonged to your grandfather with whom you were very close but who passed away. Playing with these clubs allows you to maintain that sacred bond the two of you shared. If you can summon a tear or two it will really drive home this point. Now let's see your partner tell you to buy new clubs. A caveat here: do not use this excuse on family!

C.     *Borrowed or Rented Clubs*

As I mentioned previously in Chapter 3.E, I once had the great fortune of playing TPC Sawgrass. And, as I made it clear, the weather was not cooperative. Having constantly checked the weather leading up to my flight from New York to Jacksonville and being confident that we would not be playing, I decided not to bring my clubs with me. When my friend's father-in-law told me we were definitely playing, I pointed out one slight issue that I might face: I had no clubs. Not to worry, he had his old set that he had just stopped using because he recently purchased new clubs. Fantastic.

There was only one problem with these clubs; they were so old I could have sworn that Old Tom Morris played with them. I could not hit these clubs to save my life, and even when I did connect they went about 75% as far as they should have. In order to control the ball flight I had to take shorter swings. It was not until the fourth hole that I finally hit a fairway. The wedges were much easier to hit for some reason, so I played semi-respectably. In fact, I did not even need to use any of the 200 some odd excuses I had lined up for the famous 17$^{th}$-hole island green. Yes, I am proud to say that I did not go into the water. I landed safely on the walkway that leads players onto the island green, chipped on made my par. Of course, after I hit the walkway, I made sure to turn to my friend's father-in-law and the others in the group and point out, for the 50$^{th}$ time that day, that I needed to play this course with my own clubs because I am sure I would do much better. These old clubs definitely added 6-7 strokes to my score, if not more (I did not want to overly exaggerate because, after all, this guy had given me clubs and paid for my round). Naturally, though, every time I laid out that excuse, he countered with, "I've played with those clubs for years and I never had a problem." "Well of course not," I responded, "you are used to them. This is my first time playing with them."

Much like borrowed clubs, rented clubs are unfamiliar and likely will not feel comfortable in your hand. Moreover, depending on the course that you are playing, they may be pieces of garbage. I remember I once played a round at a course where I had to rent clubs. I had not anticipated golfing that weekend, but my wife apparently dreaded the idea of spending an entire day with me, so she sent me out to the course. When I asked the gentleman in the pro-shop if he had a rental set, I was told they had a "hodge-podge." I thought to myself, "Well, this should be interesting." The bag I was given had a driver made of wood, two 5-woods (one Callaway and one Ping), old 3, 4, 7 and 9 irons from Callaway, a new Titleist 8-iron, a Cleveland wedge and a semi-new Scotty Cameron putter. Keep in mind that, at this time, I had never played with any clubs other than King Cobras or the Old Tom Morris clubs I mentioned in the previous paragraph. I had so many excuses in this bag my head almost exploded. No one could deny that my driver left me at a huge disadvantage. Maybe Ben Hogan could hit a wooden driver, but no way could I. The irons all had different feels to them and my distances were off all day. Forget about putting. I had NO FEEL. There were all tailor-made excuses for every shot that day, a dream excuse scenario for when a bad round crops up.

Unlike the dream-excuse scenario I encountered, more often than not you will receive a complete set of respectable clubs as a rental set. In this case, your excuses are not club specific, but rather bag specific. Unless you end up playing with the exact same type of clubs you normally play with, you will have grip issues, distance issues, feel issues, ball flight issues, spin issues, touch problems around the green, and of course, the putter will not be as responsive to your normally solid putting stroke. The essential component here is, after each missed shot, start your sentences with, "If I had my normal clubs..." or "Well, with my regular clubs that would have..." This way, you constantly drive home the fact that you are playing with clubs outside of your comfort zone. The added benefit, as with most excuses in this chapter, is that your playing partners will look at your good shots with even more respect because you were able to pull the shot off without your normal clubs.

D.      *Missing Clubs*

Anyone that has ever practiced in their garage, backyard, basement or apartment has likely left a club at home and not realized it until it is too late. While this is always disappointing, it is also an opportunity to take advantage of a sure-fire excuse. My Nike Slingshots did not come with a sand wedge, so I figured I would just use my old sand wedge until I replaced it. The only problem was that my Nikes were delivered to my apartment in Manhattan and my old clubs were at my parents' house. I usually hit my gap wedge 115 yards, my sand wedge 90 yards and my lob wedge 60 yards. Without my sand wedge, there was a rather large distance gap to overcome. Perhaps this would not be an issue for a more proficient golfer, but it was for me.

I think that first round with my new clubs and no sand wedge I faced a 90 yard shot on 19 holes (that might be a slight exaggeration, but I had that shot a lot). The first few times I tried to really lay into a lob wedge, which predictably did not go over well. I skulled it a couple of times and chunked it a few others. It's never fun to hit lob wedge twice in a row from 90 yards out. After the failed lob wedge experiments, I tried to lay off my gap wedge. Taking a half swing with a club is not incredibly difficult, but to take 20-25 yards off a club is quite challenging. A common swing mistake that occurs when you try to take distance off of a shot is either hitting a very loose shot or skulling the ball. Over the next few holes I managed to do both.

Thankfully, I knew these results were distinct possibilities, so I began my excuse preparation immediately upon arriving at the first tee. Before I even needed my sand wedge, I made a big show of looking at my bag and not seeing my wedge and threw a few expletives in when I realized it was "at home". Then, before each shot that required a sand wedge, I would say, "Normally I'd hit my sand wedge here. Um, I have no clue how to hit this shot now, but I'll give it a try." After each failed attempt a simple, "Damn I wish I had my freaking sand wedge" was all that was needed.

Similar situations can arise in the event a club breaks during your round. In The Masters in 2007, Tiger Woods hit a tee shot on the 11th hole that landed at the base of a tree. For his next shot he hit a great recovery with his 4-iron. Unfortunately, his 4-iron did not survive. His club smashed against a pine tree and broke in half. Of course, he is Tiger Woods, so he went on to make par at one of the hardest par-4's in all of golf. Not every golfer, however, can maintain the mental composure needed to turn such a loss into a gain. Most will crumble and let the frustration overtake their game to the point where there will be no good shots to speak of and so many bad shots that even this book cannot save you—unless you stay focused.

A few holes later, Tiger and his caddy, Steve Williams, were standing over his ball in the middle of the fairway. Steve told Tiger the ball was the perfect distance for a 4-iron. Tiger stared at Steve with confusion and Steve realized they did not have a 4-iron, so he said Tiger should just hit a strong 5, which he did. For the rest of us, we arrive at the same scenario as I had with my lack of a sand wedge. Whether you decided to skull a shorter iron or hit a longer one fat, remember that your poor shot was the tree's fault, and make sure blame is placed on the appropriate cause.

One quick cautionary tale here. I was playing a round of golf one summer morning with two brothers. The younger one had just purchased a new driver that he proceeded to slice on four of the first five holes (the one he did not slice was a mid-length par 3). When we got to the sixth hole he badly sliced his tee shot, again. What happened next was surreal. Unable to control his anger, he snapped his brand new driver over his knee and threw it deep into the woods. His brother and I stood there speechless.[3] The ninth hole on this course is a long, uphill par-5 that just so happens to be the number one handicap. He had to hit three-wood off the tee and could only muster a double-bogey 7. As we walked off the green, he was complaining that he just did not have the distance necessary for that hole. To which his brother replied, "Maybe if you weren't such a moron and didn't break your driver, you could have bogeyed it." Only a brother (or my father) could say such a thing. The point here is, if you want to use a broken club as an excuse, try not to be the one that purposely broke it because the excuse, while valid, opens you up to many a comeback.

*E.        Other Equipment Issues*

Clubs, whether they are new, old, broken or missing, are not the only equipment related issues that one encounters on a golf course. Every round of golf that I play with new shoes allows me to complain that my feet are uncomfortable. Coincidentally,

---

[3] Side note: Had I messed up at any point on this hole, I would have used the excuse that his antics threw me off my game. Thankfully, I am too proficient to let something so odd distract me.

every bad shot I hit comes at a time when I am suffering from this discomfort. Also, new shoes can cause blisters and blisters can cause slices, hooks, topped shots and more often than anything else, inaccuracy on short putts. The great thing about these shoe/foot related excuses is that people will not want to look at your feet, so they cannot challenge the validity of such an excuse.

There are other shoe-related issues that can arise. I once played a round of golf on the Black Course at Bethpage State Park in particularly heavy shoes. For those of you who have not played Bethpage Black, not only is it one of the most difficult courses on the planet, but you are not permitted to take a golf cart. Thus, walking this behemoth of a course (7,000 yards uphill the whole time, except for four tee shots) is already difficult; but, playing in the heavy shoes I was in made it even more difficult. I consistently told the three people I was grouped with that my feet were killing me. I took every opportunity to sit down. Some people may call this whining, I call it committing to the role. Honestly, though, those shoes were really heavy so I never wore them again, seriously. What, you don't believe me?

One piece of equipment that is incredibly vital to the game, but which can cause innumerable problems is the golf ball. Players find a ball they like and will stick with it for as long as the ball is sold. When I first started playing this was not a huge issue because I bought the cheapest balls I could find. But, after I started to realize that balls offered a great excuse, I started buying certain types, experimenting with different balls to procure different excuses. Two piece balls are harder and thus offer less control on putts. Three piece balls are softer but may not travel as far. Certain balls have larger dimples for distance and others have smaller dimples for feel and spin. Whatever the type of ball you are playing on a particular day, it is imperative that you understand the benefits that the ball design provides, and when the exact opposite occurs, you know it is the ball's design that caused the error.

Additionally, there are also problems unique to certain specialty balls. Yellow balls are distracting and cause slices and hooks. Night play balls light up when they are hit so they can be located easier; however, the material is such that distance control is near impossible and bad approach shots are guaranteed. Also, certain balls that my mother has purchased have been either deaf or stubborn because she says they do not respond to her vocal commands. Finally, it is a little known fact that certain manufacturers insert magnets into their balls that are attracted to water so that you lose balls quicker and have to buy more, hence increasing their profits. Plus, if nothing else, it is always fun to say, "My balls are killing me" and not be talking dirty.

## 5. COURSE RELATED EXCUSES

*A.     Playing a New Course*

There is no easier act than pleading ignorance. In golf, unlike in life, this is a completely plausible and semi-respectable excuse. Every hole at a new golf course lays before you a fresh set of excuses. Some courses play longer than their yardage because they are uphill. Others are confounding because of hidden pitfalls.

Before my parents finally moved to Florida, they rented a house for several years at PGA National Resort & Spa, home to five golf courses. When I made my maiden voyage to visit them during January of 2002, I was joyfully unattached (that one will probably cost me a night of sleeping on the couch) and thus able to play every single day I was there. One day I was set to play an early round by myself and 18-holes later in the day with my parents. I stepped to the first tee of the Haig Course and, having never played this course before, asked the starter for any tips he might have for the hole. He said, "If you feel confident you can avoid the water, take it out that way" and he pointed over a water trap that did not look to far to carry.

So I sent my tee shot soaring over the water hazard to a blind landing area. More than content with my shot, I wished him good day and was on my way, sure that I would be able to reach this medium length par-5 in two after such a tremendous tee shot. When I rounded the edge and did not see a ball, I was not happy. I was even more upset when I saw water on the other side of the fairway. Not having any idea that there was water there, I dropped a ball with utter disgust and disdain. Unfortunately, I was playing alone, so my perfect excuse of not knowing the course would have to wait until I recounted my round to my parents at lunch. Nonetheless, the excuse still "holds water" (poor pun, I know).

More recently, I played a round of golf with my father at my parents' new club. Having never played there before, when we arrived at the par-4 7th hole, I asked my father how far the water was from the tee. He said it was unreachable. After my tee shot rolled into the water, I looked at him completely flabbergasted, "I thought you said it was unreachable." "It is, I have never reached it," he replied grinning ear to ear, "You're laying three." Thus, the joys of playing a course you have never played.

Now some people will tell you to play it safe if you are not sure of how far it is to a hazard. To this I say, bah humbug. If you want to go for it, go for it and know that having never played the course before is a totally legitimate excuse. If you are playing with someone and they do not accept that excuse, it is completely fair to blame them instead. If they had been either more precise with what little information they provided or spoken up when they saw you take driver with water well within reach, then they are the proper target of your wrath.

B.     *Blame the Groundskeeper*

The layout and design of a course are not the only physical attributes that can cause fits for a player. At U.S. Open courses, rough is commonly known to be grown as high a 4 inches; instead of using a club, even the pros would appreciate being able to carry a weed whacker in their bag. During the 2006 U.S. Open at Winged Foot Golf Club, needing only par on the 72$^{nd}$ hole to win his third major, Phil Mickelson drove his tee shot into the rough and could not advance the ball out of the deep grass. He went on to make double-bogey and finish in a three-way tie for second place. Afterwards, Phil was quoted as saying, "I still am in shock that I did that. I just can't believe that I did that. I am such an idiot." Don't feel too bad for poor old Phil, he still took home nearly $500,000 in his losing effort and got to play Winged Foot for free without being a member.

Of course, if I won $500,000 each time I double-bogeyed a hole because of the rough, I would probably be just as magnanimous and take the blame just as Phil did. However, since I do not receive any money, my reward is blaming something other than myself. In the case of overgrown rough, it is not enough to just complain the grass is too thick. After all, whose fault is it that the grass grew? God's? Well you can feel free to blame God; I will stick to someone with a little less clout in the universe: the grounds crew.

When you find yourself searching for your tee shot by stomping around in ankle-high grass hoping to step on the ball (and possibly sprain an ankle in the process), remember that the grounds crew has lawn mowers, but they chose to mess with you. They could have cut the grass down to below U.S. Open height, but they hate you. So, when you hit your ball 35-feet, are you to blame? Absolutely not. You are a wonderful person that would never harm a fly, unless it was sitting on your ball when you are getting ready to swing. If the grounds crew has some deranged baseless vendetta against you, your golf score should not suffer. But, what should happen, is that anytime you land in the rough, you should point out how incredibly deep it is and that if you wanted to play U.S. Open style rough you would have reserved a tee time at a U.S. Open course. The nice thing here, again, is that this excuse can be used by everyone in your group, so it is unlikely anyone will call you out on this since they may want to use the excuse later in the round.

Alternatively, if you are playing at a course that you frequent, you can try this doosey that someone gave me once. We were on the third hole when my playing partner finally missed the fairway off the tee (miraculously, I had hit all three thus far). After he hit his 6-iron approximately 40 feet, he looked at me and said, "I cannot believe he actually did this to me." Naturally, I looked around. When I saw nobody near us, I just assumed this man was clinically insane and that I would have to use my 9-iron as a defensive weapon at some point in the round.

That's when he unleashed one of the great excuses of all time, "I was here last week and I hit one of the groundskeepers with my tee shot. When I got to my ball he was standing there looking all pissy and asked why I did not yell fore. I told him that I did not see him and besides, he had a construction hat on so what was the big deal. That's when he told me that he knew I played here a lot and he was going to grow the grass out just to piss me off." A moment before I was going to call 9-1-1 to inform them that I had located an escaped mental asylum patient, it hit me that I could actually use this to my advantage. On the next hole, when I chunked my green-side chip, I turned to him and said, "That's your fault. If you didn't piss off the grounds crew, I would have had a much better lie."

Long rough is not the only cause for poor shots on the golf course. There are many condition-related excuses that you can rely on. For poorly manicured courses, the rough can be uneven, causing your ball to unfairly land in an area of thick rough surrounded by more closely trimmed areas. The next time you are in this situation, after you chunk your shot look right at your partner and say, "Well that shouldn't count because the grass around my ball was uneven. Really, I was just doing the grounds crew's job by leveling the grass." The great thing about this is that after your shot, all the evidence will be gone so your partner cannot dispute your claim (unless you skull it and fail to do any excavating whatsoever).

It is not just the rough that can cause problems. You can encounter dried out fairways that inhibit a precision golfer such as yourself. Additionally, some course's fairway can pose very unique issues. As mentioned earlier, when I started golfing I played the local course in my town, Tamarack Golf Course. Being a county course and basically having a monopoly at the time, the county put little, if any, money into course upkeep. One of the side effects was that the course was overrun by geese. While the goose-droppings caused serious issues, I do not have the stomach to relive the memories those landmines sticking to my ball, causing bad rolls or causing uneven footing. My friends and I always had a goose excuse that could be used by any person, on any hole, at any time. However, you do not need to have geese for this excuse to work, any animal will do. All you have to say is that you hit the ball wherever you did to avoid the specific animal type, be it goose, gator, snake or otherwise. If anyone attempts to challenge you on this, simply inform them that you firmly believe all animals should be treated with respect, which is why you belong to the ASPCA or PETA—bonus points if you actually join one of these organizations and have a member card you can show to your playing partner (remember, it is called committing to the role).

This excuse will work as long as you do not actually hit an animal, which, sadly I did once (do not worry, both animal and my score were uninjured, though the goose made out better than my scorecard). I say it was sad because after this event my buddy never let me use the "avoiding the goose" excuse again, which is why we stopped playing together as much. It was one of my first rounds ever and I was playing at Tamarack. For the most part my ball never got too high off of the ground. On the fourth hole, my ball was sitting in the middle of the fairway, so I lined up my approach with my 5-iron. I took a swing, not a good swing mind you, but a swing nonetheless. The ball never got airborne, but it was traveling fast enough to go over 150 yards. Unfortunately, there was a family of geese in the middle of the fairway and my ball ran right in between a baby goose's legs. It essentially made him do a back-flip. I felt terrible, but like a trooper, he shook it off and kept going. My ball definitely lost momentum though, and instead of reaching the green came up short causing me to rely on a non-existent short game. After I wrote down the snowman on my scorecard, I looked at my buddy and said, "That damn baby goose cost me at least one stroke there, maybe two." He just looked at me in awe; I think he bought it, but I am not sure because he just turned and walked away.

C.     *Other Course Employees*

On any given day, people perform their jobs and other routine activities with others watching. However, on a golf course people watching you perform will actually cause a mistake. This is a scientific fact that I have been able to prove by playing thousands of rounds of golf with people other than myself. Now, while you should feel free to blame your playing partners for looking at you and causing a duff, remember they will be with you for your entire round and golf is supposed to be cordial and dignified, so blaming one of them might not be the best form. Therefore, this section will instead focus on a few other people that can throw you off: course rangers; the starter; and, caddies.

1.     Rangers

The following situation has no doubt happened to us all. Setting up to hit your approach shot from the middle of the fairway you see a golf cart coming at you from out of the trees. The cart's driver stops on the car path next to the green to allow you to hit your approach without seeing the cart moving. You look back down at the ball and take your swing, sending that tiny flying orb directly into the woods 100 feet to your left. Great. So now what?

Now you blame the ranger. Sure he stopped silently parked out of site so as to not distract you, but he's there isn't he? He just sits there looking at you wondering why you are slowing up play on his golf course. No doubt he is a curmudgeon whose only joy in life comes from screwing with your golf game. Always remember, it was his fault not yours.

My mother is convinced that in order to be hired as a ranger one must prove to the club's ownership that he is a rude, sexist male. She believes this even though the husband of one of her good friends, who is one of the sweetest men alive, was a ranger.[4] I remember one round I was playing with my parents down at the Jersey shore. After my father and I teed off on the $8^{th}$ hole my mom drove up to the ladies tees. It was at that point that the ranger appeared from over the hill. He stopped and watched my mom tee off. Her ball went about 30-40 feet. She picked up her tee in a huff and stormed back to the cart. We were right behind her when she looked, or rather glared at us, and said, "Goddamn ranger, I just knew he was gonna say something to me so I was not concentrating."

---

[4] I say "was a ranger" because he only lasted one day before he quit. Turns out he could not admonish slow golfers. On his first day, his supervisor told him to drive up to a foursome of slow golfers and tell them that they needed to pick up the pace of play. He drove right over to them and, wagging his finger at them violently, asked, "How you guys enjoying your round?" He then told them to have a nice day and drove off.

She drove towards her ball (it was not a long drive) and my father and I drove towards the ranger. He greeted us, complimented my father on his drive and told us to have a nice day. But, as any smart husband and son would do, we choose not to inform my mother that he was actually a nice guy. We did this for two reasons: (1) we know better than to correct an angry woman; and (2) her excuse, while unfounded, was still legitimate. I would be remiss if I did not point out that you can only use this excuse when the ranger is around, so if one shows up you might want to purposely (as far as your partners are concerned) hit a bad shot just to "test" this excuse—hey look, that's another good excuse, testing an excuse. So, the next time you see a ranger on your hole, take solace in knowing that it is his fault you hit a bad shot, and that he is likely a sexist bastard.

### 2. Caddies

I have only played with a caddy a few times in my life, so my experience here is not overwhelming. Nonetheless, I learned some very important things about playing with a caddy. First and foremost, they do not like it when you blame them for your bad shots. I did not do this, but I guy I was playing with did and his caddy was none too thrilled with him. The other thing I learned was that they are more than willing to accept the blame for your mistakes (provided you are nice to them) if it means you save face with your partners (plus, this usually results in a bigger tip, so they are on board).

I will venture a guess that everyone reading this book predominately plays their golf without employing a caddy. That being the case, you are all fairly adept at choosing a club for your shot, knowing where to hit the ball, where not to hit the ball (unless it is your first time playing the course, in which case make sure to read Chapter 5.A again) and of course, reading a green. The immediately preceding sentence notwithstanding, when we hire a caddy for a round we expect them to handle all of these duties for us so that we can simply concentrate on making a solid and consistent swing.

Imagine you are standing over your ball with 150 yards to the pin. Normally you would hit your 8-iron, but your caddy talks you into a 7-iron. Regardless of whether you skull your shot over the green or chunk it short, as you walk to your ball, feel free to announce to anyone listening that your caddy mis-clubbed you. Should your partner have the audacity to ask why you did not overrule the club selection, all you have to do is inform him that you are much too polite for such a confrontation and you instead thought you would take a little off the shot. Notice the subtle interplay between this excuse, blaming the caddy, and the excuse for being in-between clubs (Chapter 4.D). Never be afraid, when appropriate, to commingle excuses.

Not only can a caddy give you the wrong club, but he or she could also read a green improperly. When you miss a putt because your caddy told you to aim three inches left but there was no break at all, blame your caddy. When talking to your playing partner on your way to the next hole, quietly say, "He told me to play it outside left, but that thing was dead straight. He works here, he should really know the greens better than that." It is a compelling argument, never mind that you crushed your putt through the break and ended up 6 feet past the hole. The same "he should know" excuse also works when you hit your ball into a hazard that you could not see. Had your caddy told you that 200 yards left of the green there is a swimming pool in someone's backyard, then you would not have hit your ball there.

Let me now provide one excuse that can be used following your round. This is a time-sensitive excuse, in that you can only use it after your first round with a caddy, unless the people you are talking to do not know you have used a caddy before. The first time I played with a caddy, I was really nervous. I did not really want a caddy, but the course rules required that any non-member must be accompanied by one. So I was standing on the first tee and this old guy came over and said he was my caddy. Fantastic! It was almost 90 degrees and this old guy, wearing a jump suit was going to have to lug my golf bag around for 4 ½ hours. I wanted to carry the bag for him I felt so bad.

Now, after a while that feeling dissipated, but I held onto it. I stored it in my memory bank. Then, when my parents and fiancée asked me how my round was I made sure to start off by letting them know, in great detail, about my caddy. I told them how he almost had a stroke on the 4th hole, how he had to take a rest during the long par-5 7th hole and how he barely made through the back nine. I told them about how on the 17th tee he could not bend down to pick up grass to gauge the wind. And after all that, I told them that I shot a 92 but it could have been an 85 had I not been so distracted and distraught by his suffering.

## 6. PHYSICAL AND EMOTIONAL EXCUSES

Some of the most commonly used excuses on a golf course relate to injuries or general health. Far too often, however, the amateur golfer will not expand their horizons beyond the basic excuse. This chapter addresses the basics, but as with any good instruction manual, goes beyond the basics and explores more advanced topics.

*A. Physical Injuries*

As I begin writing this chapter, I am undergoing physical therapy on my knee. I have been having knee issues for several years and when a tourist's suitcase fell into my knee on the subway and bent it the wrong way, the knee went from achy to seriously hurt in a nanosecond.[5] In any event, since my knee has been balky, I have already been planning my excuses for upcoming rounds. To my dismay, my favorite golfer of all time has attempted to throw a wrench in the works. It seems that after finishing second to Trevor Immelman in The Masters in 2008, Tiger Woods had arthroscopic knee surgery. Apparently, he had been playing for the past several weeks with a bum knee but played through the pain because he is such a fierce competitor.[6]

---

[5] A quick note to all of you who have never been on a subway before; when the train starts to move HOLD ONTO YOUR BAGS!
[6] After finishing this book but before actually getting it published Tiger further cramped my style by winning the US Open with a broken leg.

Since none of us are on the PGA we do not need to worry about allowing our playing competitors to gain confidence from the knowledge that we are playing hurt. In fact, we are better off with our partners knowing this information so that they will feel sorry for us and be more accepting of our excuses. Personally, I plan to buy a huge brace, crutches and maybe even get the course to provide one of those little yellow flags that means I can drive my cart all the way up to the green.

The key is to make sure your injury is well-known and evokes sympathy. Make sure you grimace a lot and by all means, feel free to moan or scream after a poor shot. In addition, you should always bring a bottle of Alleve or Advil to the course with you. The nice thing about Advil is that you can take 4 of them and they will not upset your stomach, so if your group does not see you take the first two then take another two when you are sure they are looking. On the other hand, Alleve can upset your stomach, but you can play that to your advantage. At the turn, or when you see the food cart, make sure to tell your partners that you need food in order to take the Alleve "needed to get rid of the pain in my [*fill in the body part of your choice*] and get through the round."

After I graduated law school, I lived with my friend Brett for a couple of years. Brett was an accomplished high school athlete, albeit in a not-so-athletic high school. Having entered the business world but still clinging to his glory days, Brett and his office-mates joined a softball league in Central Park. Apparently in one of these games Mr. Athlete broke, or at the very least, severely injured his coccyx bone (that means his butt). I mention this because during that time we would play golf together frequently. He came in from the game and told me what happened and, after I stopped laughing, I realized he was probably just laying the foundation for another butt-whopping (gotta love those puns) that weekend in golf. Sure enough we played and every time he hit a bad shot he would wince and grab his backside. This excuse also gave me an excuse; after all, do you have any idea how hard it is to play golf when you are laughing so hard that it hurts?

In fairness to me, there was a time when I had some injury issues during a round of golf and Brett handled it the same way that I handled his broken butt (that may have come out wrong…let's just move on). I had a hernia and every time I took a misstep, stubbed my toe or contorted my body in the wrong way, it caused excruciating pain. While suffering from this injury, we played at a very hilly golf course in Long Island. On the 10th hole my drive went well right into the woods and came to rest on a fairly severe side-hill lie. When I took my swing my club hit a tree root and I fell over. I was in so much pain I nearly vomited—Brett laughed. For the next few holes, every bad shot

I hit was a product of the searing pain I felt from that shot on 10. More importantly, every good shot was hit in spite of the pain because I am such a competitor.

Knee injuries, hernias or even a broken butt are not the only physical ailments you can suffer on a golf course. Regardless of whether you stub your toe getting out of bed in the morning (a known cause of yips in putts) or hurt your neck because you slept funny (scientifically proven to cause hooks or slices depending on which side of your neck hurts), the important thing is to make sure that injury is public knowledge. Sure it may be embarrassing in most social settings to tell people your butt is broken, but on a golf course it is critical to the ability to establish a proper and valid excuse.

*B. Not Feeling Well*

When you are sick the most important thing you can do is skip work and go play a round of golf (I hope my boss does not read this book). Some people, like those pesky doctors, will tell you to stay home, lie in bed, get lots of rest and take your medicine. I say, rarely do you get the opportunity to use this excuse on a golf course, so you should take advantage.

Several years ago, I went golfing with my mother and two of her friends. I was not feeling particularly well, but it was a free round of golf so obviously I was not passing that up. During the car ride to the course I was fairly quiet, mostly because I was in a car with my mom and her two friends who only wanted to gossip. When they asked me why I was so quiet, I let them know that I was not feeling great—foundation laid.

During the round I had less energy than normal and it affected my ability to put a solid swing together for the entire round. Each time I hit a loose shot I would stand over my divot for several seconds and use the club as a brace. In between holes I would sit on the benches or stay in the cart; one time I even closed my eyes to catch some shut-eye while the women teed off. After thirteen holes, we arrived at the green of the par-5 14th hole. Having reached the green in regulation, I was still about 80 feet from the hole. I hit my putt to about five feet and proceeded to sit down on the green. When they asked if I was okay, I calmly responded, "I am just so tired, I cannot believe I could not reach the hole on that putt." They felt so bad that they gave me the putt. PAR!

On 15 I hit my tee shot out of bounds and before I could even say anything, one of my mom's friends said, "Oh, Jason, that's okay, you're not feeling well. You should try to hit another one, no penalty." I've said it before, and I will say it again, you must buy into your excuse and sell it with the acting. Just saying you are sick is not enough; you need to convince the others you are playing with of your ailment.

## C. Allergies

Nothing is better than being out on a golf course, in the middle of nature surrounded by green grass, trees and assorted species of plants and animals. If you agreed with that sentence, then you are probably not an allergy sufferer. For those of you who read that sentence and started to have tears in your eyes or began getting an itchy feeling all over, then this section is for you. The only drawback of golf, other than the maddening inability to play flawlessly leading to a surging desire to smash yourself or others with a wedge, is that golf is played outdoors.

For most of the population, being outdoors equals suffering from allergies. In fact, the allergy business is a multi-billion dollar a year industry because of the fact that nearly everyone suffers from some sort of allergy. The good thing about allergies is that they are so commonplace that telling someone you are an allergy sufferer will not raise any eyebrows. In general, you are better off sticking with the primary allergy symptoms, such as watery eyes, running nose and itchiness, as opposed to something extreme, such as swollen fingers or a closed esophagus. After all, it is a lot easier to rub your eyes and turn them red then it is to make your fingers plump up (however, if you know how to spontaneously make your fingers plump up, maybe you should have a show in Vegas, then you could play all year long and always have the heat-related excuses at your disposal).

So how do you take your affliction and turn it into something positive? It is easy. Have you ever tried to hit a golf ball with your eyes closed? Maybe you have on the driving range, but not on the course, because you know how difficult this can be.[7] Well, there is very little difference between hitting a ball with your eyes closed and hitting the ball with water in your eyes. If your eyes are teary from allergies you will not be able to maintain solid and consistent visual contact with the ball. So the next time your shot does not go exactly the way you want, just let your partners know, "Hey, that was the best I could expect considering my allergies are killing me and I could not see the ball because my eyes were tearing up."

There is a simple, yet far too often overlooked, aspect of this excuse that must be attended to in order for it to be believable: you must have tears in your eyes. It is one thing to blame watery eyes when you actually have watery eyes, but to try to blame watery eyes when they are bone dry, well even I cannot condone

---

[7] Of course, many instructors will tell you that there is no difference between hitting the ball with your eyes open versus closed. This is because the ball is not moving, so if you set up to the ball properly, you should be able to make the same swing whether your eyes are open or closed. Of course, this assumes the golf ball will go directly where you are aiming. Since we know that won't be the case, you will need your eyes open so that you can see if it goes into the trees, water or someone's backyard.

that, unless you have a rare eye disorder whereby the water in your eye drips into your head instead of out of your eye socket (hmm, that could be an interesting one to add to the list, I will have to look it up). If your eyes are not cooperating, try one of these two approaches: (1) pluck a few eyelashes or (2) rub your eyes until they are red and watery.

One of the easiest set ups for this excuse arises when the grounds crew is cutting, or recently cut, the grass. Freshly cut grass can always lead to allergy flare-ups. But, even if there are no fresh grass clippings, that does not mean your very sensitive nose cannot sense that grass was cut at some point within the last month. And, those grass clippings have clearly been irritating your throat making you want to cough and sneeze incessantly. However, out of respect for your fellow golfer, you have restrained your urges. Unfortunately, a sneeze tried to force its way out causing a momentary lapse in concentration leading you to skull that last lob wedge 130 yards even though you were only 65 yards from the green. Sounds fairly plausible, right? Well it should, because that exact scenario happened to me once and you should feel free to use my misfortune to your benefit.

Watery eyes and sneezes are not the only allergic reactions possible on a golf course. Perhaps you are very itchy as a result of the course's unique vegetation (yes, dandelions can be considered unique). This itchiness no doubt distracted you during your last swing when, instead of focusing on keeping your head down, you attempted to rid yourself of that itch on your nose by twitching your face. Trust me, that twitching led you to top your drive off the tee instead of crushing a 280 yard bomb with a slight fade.

Having an allergic reaction to nature is not the only allergy-related excuse to be aware of. You can have an allergic reaction to the food you ate at the turn and that food allergy can rear its head during the back nine. Personally, I am allergic to the pesticides found in the skin of fruit. Seriously, I am, stop laughing! Anyway, whenever I eat a fruit such as an apple, plum or pear, I become extremely itchy, get watery eyes and my throat starts to scratch. You would think that if I knew I was allergic to fruit skin that I would not eat it, well you would be wrong. Sometimes I just pop some fruit into my mouth without even thinking (one of the many reasons why my wife tells me I am an idiot). I remember one time I was playing with my parents in the middle of the afternoon. I did not get any food at the turn, but around the 12$^{th}$ hole I started to get hungry. Like a boy scout, my mom always comes prepared and when I told her I was hungry, she offered me a fresh plum. Well, it took about two bites before I remembered why I don't eat fruit. I got itchy all over and no matter how much water I drank, I could not get rid of that scratchy feeling in my throat. I stepped to the tee on the 12$^{th}$ hole at Sea Oaks, a 210-yard par three with a waste bunker from tee to green on the left side. I almost exploded trying to hold it together through my swing. To this day I am not sure where that ball landed. I swear it went in the hole, but my father tells me it went backwards. We split the difference and I dropped the ball in the sand greenside. Two lessons should be taken here. First, food allergies are just as culpable for poor swings as any other allergy. Second, don't ever rely on my father to tell you where you ball went.

## D. *Have to go to the Bathroom*

Any round I play with my mother at any course inevitably contains the exact same conversation. Ninety-nine times out of a hundred it follows my mom rushing herself through a putt or a tee shot and not being happy with the result. She will look up at me and say, "Okay that was not my fault. I'm going to the bathroom. I'll meet up with you in a minute." Then I respond, "Yes, mom" (I am such a good son). We have this conversation even when I treat her like a child and make sure she goes before we leave the house. Put simply, I think she has the smallest bladder known to man, sorry WO-man. When she plays a course for the first time, she always comments on the location and abundance of bathrooms on the course. In fact, when my parents were looking into joining a golf club, this was one of her biggest concerns.

Regardless of the size of your bladder, you should take a lesson from my mother. Having to "go potty" as my mom puts it, can seriously influence your swing. After all, it is difficult enough to maintain balance normally, but trying to maintain balance **and** do the potty dance at the same time is a near impossibility.

Whether you actually need to go to the bathroom or just hit a poor shot and need an excuse, a full bladder is always plausible. However, this book is about more than just providing the excuse, it is about implementation. So, as with any excuse the devil is in the details. Biologically, the bladder resides just below your navel. Therefore, if you want to complain that your full bladder caused you to rush your swing, make sure you do not grab your leg when giving this excuse. Similarly, the bladder is in the front half of your body. Thus, grabbing your buttocks while telling your partner that you had to go pee will confuse her to no end (though that confusion could be useful in competition).

Now, when your bladder is full there will be added pressure and/or weight in the front part of your body. This will inevitably cause you to lean slightly forward, thus ruining your balance. With the weight improperly placed too far over your feet, you are likely to chunk your shot. Instead of getting angry after such an occurrence, simply turn to your partner and with a bit of strain to sell the point, say, "I had to pee so bad there was no way I could hit that shot. The fact that I made contact at all without wetting my pants is a miracle." If they attempt to quiz you on this issue, explain to them the physical placement of the bladder in the body and the result of the full bladder. Even if they do not believe you, at least they will think you are really smart.

A full bladder will also prevent you from bending over properly out of fear that you might release more than just your hips early, if you get my drift. In other words, a full bladder could also cause you to stand taller than you should during a particular shot. Standing upright will result in topped shots and skulls. Thus, a topped or skulled shot should be followed by an immediate question to your opponents, "Hey, do you know where the closest bathroom is? Now my bladder is affecting my game."

One final note on this topic before we move on. For all you guys (and I guess you uncouth women), while you may think relieving yourself in the woods helps water the plants, just know that it removes your ability to rely on this excuse once you are done peeing. But, if you really must go this route, just make sure you take stock of which way the wind is blowing before you start going.

*G. Drunk on the Course*

Golf is an extremely unique sport in that a large segment of the golfing community actually drinks while playing. People's reasoning for drinking on the course vary from celebratory rounds (e.g., bachelor parties), to excessive temperatures, to medicinal purposes (e.g., curing a hangover). Whatever the reason and whatever the amount consumed, alcohol provides an inordinate number of potential excuses. Even if you are not imbibing an exorbitant amount, alcohol will certainly affect your play by impairing your balance, judgment and vision, and of course, leading to the need of the prior section. Due to the wide array of alcohol-related excuses possible, I thought I would share three anecdotes that illustrate how alcohol can affect your golf game, both positively and negatively.

One of my close friends got married right out of college, so when we went golfing for his bachelor party, we were all still able to hold our liquor (for the most part). During that weekend, eight of us went for a friendly round of golf. We split into two foursomes based on skill level and how serious we intended to take the round. Being in the "serious" group, we did not get completely intoxicated, but we did have a couple of drinks. Somewhere around the 13th hole, I was driving the cart pretty fast when I could have sworn that my cart-mate Scott told me to stop because he saw his ball. Well, all of the alcohol I consumed must have gone straight to my foot because I slammed on the break pretty hard. Scott was leaning forward at the time and proceeded to fly right through the Plexiglas windshield and rolled a few times on the fairway. Other than some dirtied pants and a scraped up knee, he was totally fine. That said, however, this turn of events led to a plethora of excuses, and not just for Scott who used the scraped knee as an excuse after each subsequent poor shot. Personally, I could not stop laughing during my approach shot and completely lost focus for the next few holes. Every time I stood over the ball and tried to clear my head, I had this image of Scott going through the Plexiglas.

During that same round of golf, the not-so serious guys were a few groups behind us. We were getting periodic updates from the cart girl letting us know just how much the other group was drinking, and it was a lot. However, we did not realize just how much "a lot" really meant until after the round. Being that they were three groups back, we decided to bring our clubs to the car and meet them in the parking lot. When they had not shown up 30 minutes later, we started to wonder what happened to them. Finally, they came out to the parking lot and one of the guys, Jason, was soaking wet from head to toe. Turns out that on the 16th hole Jason, who had probably had about 20 beers by then, tried to hit a sand wedge over some water to the green. We are not sure where the ball went, but his sand wedge flew out of his hand into the pond. Since these were he girlfriend's father's clubs, he was not about to lose a club, so he figured he would try go in and retrieve the wedge. He took his socks and shoes off and began to gently and slowly walk into the pond. As he put it, "my first two steps were only ankle deep. I took another few steps and the water only got to mid-calf. A few more steps and then I was knee-deep but only a few feet from where the club should have been. I took another step and apparently there was a ledge that I fell off and next thing I know I am completely under water." What was worse is that Jason was not even able to find the club, which in his words "really sucked because I was in the sand on 17 and had a short approach that was the perfect distance for a sand wedge on 18."

While the two stories above show how alcohol can impair your game, I want to share a story that proves alcohol can also improve your game. My father can be somewhat uptight at times and, even though golf is a relaxing sport, he gets even more wound up on the course. If he hits a bad shot, he will usually run after it, apparently out of fear that someone else might have hit their ball 200 yards into the woods and might mistake his ball for theirs. Sometimes he will just say "I'm out of this hole" even though there is no one behind us and the group in front of us is playing at a snail's pace giving him plenty of time to regroup. In any event, one pastime that my father enjoys as much as golf is drinking wine. He loves drinking wine, buying wine and even talking about wine. So one day, my mom and I decided to try an experiment. Before our tee time we decided to get lunch at the course's restaurant and we ordered my father a glass of wine. During the meal, we got him a second one, figuring that would mellow him out sufficiently. Well, not only was he more relaxed than usual, he also played better.

Now, you may be asking yourself why I would tell you a story about drinking that actually improved play and lessened the need for excuses. It is quite simple. For the rest of his life, my father can always blame a bad round on being sober. Think about it. How many more times do you play golf without having a drink than you do with having one? If you play 90% of your rounds without ever having a drink, that means that 90% of the time you have your failure to imbibe as an excuse. Of course, for the other 10% you can blame the alcohol for any wayward shot or, as evidenced above, physical injury or loss of a club.

*H. Heartbreak Hotel*

Physical injuries are not the only injuries that can affect your game; emotional baggage can weigh you down on a golf course just as much, if not more, than any physical injury. The best thing about emotional excuses is that they can be so sensitive that your playing partner will most likely not even question their validity. In fact, with the proper excuse, your partner may offer up the excuse before you do or might encourage you to take a mulligan.

When I was in college, a few friends and I went out for a midweek round of golf at the local course. I figured the only drama we would encounter would relate to our having missed a couple of classes (hey, it was senior year). I was wrong. Turns out my buddy had spent the prior night breaking up with his girlfriend for the third time that semester. Needless to say, he had some difficulty focusing during that round. About once every other hole he tried to bring up his ex, but we were having none of that talk. We told him to focus on his game because he was already losing money to us (not that I condone betting on golf) and he should not make it worse by thinking of his former girlfriend. Towards the end of a pretty terrible round, we all decided to let him off the hook for the money he owed us from his disastrous round. Of course, being the good friends we were, we mocked him incessantly for being so emotional.

The morals of the above anecdote are: (1) emotional issues can take a toll on your golf game; (2) such emotional issues should be highlighted during the round so that your playing partners understand the reason behind your poor play, and most importantly, (3) never tell your fraternity brothers that you are upset over having broken up with a girl.

Emotional stress can come from more than just breaking up with a significant other. I recall trying to play golf while studying for the bar exam. For those entire six weeks leading up to the bar, I think I had one good round of golf. Similarly, when my wife was in the final months of her pregnancy, I spent most of my time on the course wondering (usually aloud after a poor shot) whether she was going into labor and if I missed a phone call telling me my first child was on his way. The point is that potentially life-altering and momentous events can affect your game just as much as having to go to the bathroom or getting a poor night's sleep. Your game can also be affected by much smaller events, such as your favorite team losing a game or your kid bringing home a bad report card. As any psychologist will tell you, every event impacts our lives either positively or negatively, so the next time an event impacts your life negatively, even if it is something as small as not liking the lunch you had pre-round, be sure to turn it into a positive on the golf course by using it as an excuse for poor play.

# 7. IN SWING DISTRACTIONS

I started this book off by recounting the story of Tiger Woods at the World Golf Championship in Doral. Undoubtedly we have all experienced a similar in-swing distraction that caused a muffed shot. This chapter focuses on some of those distractions and gives some helpful tips on how to properly turn those errant shots from swing mistakes to results of an external force completely outside of your control.

## A. Other People

One of the first rules of etiquette that golfers learn, or at least are supposed to learn, is not to talk while others are swinging. This is not limited to talking to the golfer during his swing, but rather encompasses any talking to any person, animal or object. We have all been distracted at some point during one of our swings, yet for some reason this never stops people from talking or being a general nuisance while others are attempting to swing.

But, people can do more than just talk during your swing in order to provide a distraction. My father, for example, used to have this annoying habit of trying to get directly behind you so that he can track your ball for you. Two problems arise when he did this. First, he moved into your peripheral vision during your backswing, thus providing just enough of a distraction to cause you to pick your head up a fraction early. The second, and more comical, issue with his attempt is that his vision is really bad so he could not track the ball for more than about 100 yards anyway. You would think that he would stop doing this the first time he realized his vision was such that he could not see a tiny white ball against a cloudy white sky when it is traveling over 100 miles per hour. Well, you would be wrong.

I remember one time we were playing in Florida when my father got an early start on this maneuver. By the time I got to the top of my backswing, he was practically dancing right behind me. After I sliced my ball into someone's kitchen, I glared at him intently and said, "I am going to hit another one and this time I want you to stand exactly where you are and not move a single muscle. If I see you in my field of vision, I am going to turn around and aim at you." Of course, he replied, "Standing in front of you is probably the safest place I could be." I glared more intently and re-teed my ball. During my setup and practice swing I could see him inching closer and closer. I stared at him and he stopped moving. As I addressed the ball, I thought to myself, "Okay, he knows not to move, just focus and make a good swing." As I started my swing, almost as if in slow motion, I saw something creep into my field of vision. Instead of walking directly behind me, he was leaning over so that I was only able to see his head. Predictably, the ball went sailing right. As soon as I made contact he finished his maneuvering so that he was right behind me. After about 150 yards, he turned to me and said, "I lost it, but I think it was heading right." I almost had a heart attack.

## B. *Blackberry or Smartphone*

I always tell people that the best thing about having a Blackberry is the freedom that it gives me knowing that I do not have to be sitting at my desk in order for a colleague or client to find me. I immediately follow that sentiment up with the fact that the worst thing about a Blackberry is the lack of freedom I have because I do not have to be sitting at my desk in order for a colleague or client to find me.

Normally, hearing the vibration of my Blackberry means work, which means I leave whatever happy place I was then in and return to reality. Never is this truer than when I am on a golf course. Now, not all of you may have this problem, but I am a lawyer so in theory I am on call 24 hours a day. Actually, not in theory, in reality; therefore my Blackberry makes it to nearly every round of golf I play. While bringing my Blackberry to the golf course is not thrilling, I have been able to turn this negative into a positive.

At my old firm I used to take off on my birthday and hit the course for a celebratory round. One year I was playing particularly well, having shot a 39 on the front. I started the back with three straight pars and hit a solid tee shot down the middle of the fairway on the long par-5 13th hole. A line of trees and woods ran all along the left, so it was important to keep the second shot right, which also afforded the best angle to a relatively small green guarded by a bunker in front. As I started my takeaway for my second shot my Blackberry buzzed in my bag. My attention diverted, I hooked my ball into the woods, but thankfully inbounds. I figured I would chip out into the fairway for my third, get on in four and if I two-putt it would still put me at 1-over on the back through 4 holes, well on my way to my best round ever, and then I would check my email. After I chipped out, I was a mere 100 yards from the green, perfect for a nice full sand-wedge. Mid-swing my Blackberry started going nuts and my ball went well left, out of bounds. Frustrated with the turn of events and cursing my misfortune for having to work instead of winning the lottery, I proceeded to triple-bogey the hole.

The person I was playing with, who just happened to be retired, tried to console me. She told me to check my email, see what the problem was, if any, and then refocus before we teed off on 14. Naturally, the frenetic pace with which it was buzzing made me think something was wrong, well that turned out not to be the case. In actuality, I had received a mass email about the Yankees, which led to a flurry of responses from all of the recipients. Of course, instead of telling my playing partner the truth, I decided it was better off to seem important, so I just pretended it was a work issue that I easily resolved, then changed my Blackberry from vibrate to silent. On the last hole, I lipped out a chip from the fringe that would have given me a 79. I tapped in for 80 and began cursing my Blackberry as the creation from hell. In response, the woman I was playing with said, "Think about it this way, if you didn't have your Blackberry you might have had to go to the office today. And, at least it was business that distracted you and not just emails from your friends." I simply responded, "Yep. And who knew that a Blackberry vibration causes a hook."

Now, even though my Blackberry causes me to hook the ball, I have also met people who slice their shots when their Blackberry buzzes. Some people have been known to chunk chips, while others are prone to skulling approach shots. I am not sure if the difference in results is based on which service provider you use or if, perhaps, it is genetically based. What I do know, however, is that if you want to use your Blackberry as an excuse, you absolutely must remember to put it on vibrate and keep it handy. If your Blackberry is on silent and you claim to have heard it buzzing, you will most likely be given major leeway with your excuses, but only because your playing partners will think you are crazy. Likewise, if you leave your Blackberry in the car, do not blame it for your mishits; there are a plethora of other excuses in this book that you can rely on should you leave your excuse prop behind.

## C. Other Distractions

Aside from other people and technology-related disturbances, there are a whole host of distractions to be used as potential excuses during a swing; the key is to keep your eyes and ears open so that you can take advantage of an excuse when necessary. Since golf is played outdoors, except for those of you who need excuses when playing Tiger Woods Golf on PlayStation 3, the sights and sounds around you afford the not-so-talented golfer many excuses. Two personal experiences come to mind.

Several years ago (I would have said in my youth, but according to my parents, I am still young even though my wife continuously points out my grey hairs), I went to Scottsdale, Arizona with a few friends from college. Having arrived a day before my friends, I decided to play a course, We-Ko-Pa – one of the most beautiful courses I have ever played – which was recommended by the hotel concierge. Apparently, We-Ko-Pa is located close to a base for the Air Force or some other military group. Helicopters and planes frequently flew low overhead, and one helicopter in particular was circling above myself and the two gentlemen I had been paired up with that day.

I tried to put it out of my head as I stepped to the tee on the 155 yard Par-3 fifth hole, but as I stood at address, I noticed the chopper had stopped flying and was now hovering overhead. Try as I might, I could not shake the feeling that the helicopter's gunner had me in his sights, and then I proceeded to skull my tee-shot about twenty yards over the green. Having played fairly decent golf up until that point (I was one over through the first four holes), one of the guys in my group asked, "Where in the world did that come from?" Always quick on my feet, and never wanting to let someone believe I own a less than stellar golf game, I quickly responded, "That helicopter threw me off. It looked like the gunner was getting ready to shoot me or pick my ball off mid air." I believe one of the two gentlemen is still doubled over from laughter, but his friend calmly replied, "Are you some sort of secret agent that the government is after?" to which I offered, "Yes, yes I am" and then proceeded to walk to my ball.

I could have offered a number of excuses based on the chopper, but I chose to go with one of the more unusual, and I am guessing less frequently heard, excuses. If you are not as comfortable taking on the role of secret agent, then some others you could offer in a similar situation are: "I noticed the chopper in my backswing and it caused me to ever so slightly lift my head" or "The chopper's blades caused an increase in the prevailing winds and I felt I needed to swing a little harder, thus causing the inevitable topped shot."

Along a line similar to the international intrigue and mystery associated with my life as a secret agent, is another story that is somewhat more embarrassing. Several years ago I was golfing with a good friend of mine at a relatively nondescript course on Long Island. The course was a typical municipal golf course with several holes running adjacent to the backyards of various houses. Our round was progressing rather nicely that day when my buddy approached his second shot on a Par-4 running adjacent to a backyard with several kids playing together. Just as he started his club connected with the ball, one of the kids fired a toy machine gun. My friend let the club go flying out of his hand and dove to the ground hands covering his head. I too fell to the ground…laughing. Neither one of us saw where the ball ultimately ended up, but at least we were both safe: my friend was not shot and I did not pull a muscle from laughing too hard.

After we both stopped laughing, he dropped another ball and hit it into the greenside bunker, hit out of the bunker and then three-putted for a crowd-pleasing snowman. Or, at least so I thought. As he was picking his ball up out of the hole, he said, "Damn, double bogey!" I did some quick counting (using both my hands, naturally) and asked ever-so-politely, "Six, are you kidding me, in what world did you get a six?" He explained to me that there is no way he was taking a penalty shot for the ball he hit "as he was being shot at." Flabbergasted as I was, I still managed to ask, "But they weren't real bullets and seriously, who would be shooting at you anyway?" He told me that was not the point, that they could have been real bullets and he was taking a six. He's a lot bigger than me, so I gave him a six. Plus, being shot at, even if not for real, is one heck of a good excuse. One last piece of advice for those of you who happen to find yourself playing at a golf course near any type of road whatsoever, a car backfiring sounds almost exactly like a bazooka being launched in your direction.

## 8. SWING PRESSURES AND THOUGHTS

Talking or noises during your swing are not the only interferences to consider when providing an excuse for that shanked drive or yipped putt. Often times we are our own worst enemy, which reminds me of a funny line in a golf-related email I received one time: "Never try to keep more than 300 separate swing thoughts in your head at any one time."

*A. First Tee Pressure*

During one of my annual visits to Florida, my father and I played The Champion Course at PGA National Resort & Spa less than a week after it hosted The Honda Classic. Consequently, many of the grandstands were still standing. As we drove to the driving range, I joked that as long as the grandstands were up they should still have the official starter on the first tee to introduce each golfer as if we were professionals. After the driving range, I went to the practice green near the first tee for a couple of minutes. My father went to the first tee to meet his friend and the fourth golfer we were playing with. When our tee time arrived, I walked to the first tee. Since we each had a caddy, there were nine people on the tee box, plus the four people in the group behind us. As I stepped to the tee, I heard a booming voice announce, "Now on the tee, from New York, New York, Jason Frank." Apparently, my father had persuaded the starter to embarrass, I mean announce, me prior to teeing off. Well, everyone else had a nice laugh, but immediately my heart dropped to my stomach. Now I actually had to hit the ball...

*B. Pressure Putts*

As you may have surmised from some of the passages in this book, Tiger Woods is my favorite golfer. I respect, admire and secretly covet his focus, dedication and killer instinct. His ability to tune out the rest of the world and execute is something to behold. Never was this more apparent then on the 72$^{nd}$ hole of the 2008 U.S. Open at Torrey Pines. Playing on a leg that, unknown to the rest of the world, was broken in two places Tiger had a long right to left putt on a bumpy green to force an 18-hole Monday afternoon playoff with Rocco Mediate.[8] The putt bumped, skipped and hopped the entire way and when it finally dropped in the cup the entire golfing world erupted, Tiger included. The remarkable thing about that putt was not just that it went it, but that most of the people watching *expected* it to go in. It might have been one of the most pressure packed putts ever, but it was also the greatest golfer of all time stroking the putt, and it just had to drop.

---

[8] The next day Tiger went on to defeat Rocco Mediate in a 19-hole playoff and only afterward did the rest of the world learn that Tiger's leg was broken in two places and required surgery. In a meeting with his doctor prior to the U.S. Open, Tiger was told that he required surgery to repair a torn ACL and two broken bones in his leg. He told his doctor that he would have the surgery, *after he won the U.S. Open* – truly remarkable.

Unfortunately for us mere humans, we cannot simply stand there and drain an important putt with such confidence and consistency. Whether it is a friendly Nassau with your Sunday group or the club tournament, we have all had to face a scenario similar to what Tiger faced on that fateful Sunday: the Big-Money Putt. Lee Trevino has had some very poignant quotes attributed to him during his time in the public eye, two of which have always stuck with me and which bear on this portion of my book: "Putts get real difficult the day they hand out the money" and "Pressure is playing for five dollars a hole with only two in your pocket." The Big-Money Putt is rivaled only by the first tee shot of the day in the golf hierarchy or pressure shots.

If you have read this book from the beginning you have probably learned that (a) I play golf with my father frequently and (b) we like to mess with each other's heads. Thus, it should come as no surprise that whenever we play for stakes, there is an ungodly amount of trash talk that goes on between us. Despite having a handicap 13 strokes higher than mine, whenever we play together he is always at the top of his game and I normally struggle (this dates all the way back to when he used to whip my butt in ping-pong when I was a child). Quite simply, the man has ice water in his veins and it kills me. One time in particular it killed me more than normal. I was visiting my parents in Florida and playing particularly good golf that week with three consecutive rounds in the low 80's. On our final day we decided (at my request) to place a wager on our round: loser had to supply the wine for that night's dinner, two bottles of one of our favorite bottles of wine, Joseph Phelps Insignia (for you non-wine drinkers, this is perennially rated as one of the better California wines and has a price to match). Well, we all know where this is going. I played mediocre that day whereas my father, of course, played out of his mind. My father was dormie two, so as we approached the 17$^{th}$ hole, I knew I had to turn it on. I was 15 feet from the pin in two, and my dad was just off the green in three. Naturally he chips it to about a foot and taps in for a bogey. As I am lining up my downhill putt, he starts with the trash talk, "When you buy me my wine tonight, make sure it's the '97 bottle, not the '98." I told him not to get ahead of himself, all I had to do was two-putt from 15 feet and I extend the match. He laughed and started to walk away. I asked where he was going, he said, "I can't stand to watch my son three-putt from 15 feet, I'll be in the cart." Not this time, I was thinking to myself. I've got this two-putt easy and was even thinking about the 18$^{th}$ hole, a long par 4 on which my length off the tee would carry me, all I had to do was two-putt.

I don't remember how much the wine ended up costing me that night, in addition to my pride, but I do remember having to sit through all of dinner listening to my dad regale my mother and wife with the story of how I put my first putt 5 feet past the hole and then left my comeback 2 feet short. I kept telling them, and myself, over and over, "It was the nerves, they got to me. My hands were too tight on the first putt and I had no touch. Then I tried to coax the comebacker in, but it was uphill and I didn't give it enough." Of course, my ever-supportive father, reminded me that I did not have that killer instinct and often questioned my manhood…ah, the love and support of a father.

Playing for money is not the only time you can use pressure as an explanation for why you missed a putt. Pressure can arise if you are on pace to shoot the best round of your life, or quite possibly the worst. I can still vividly recall all three of my putts on the 18$^{th}$ green during the first round I ever shot in the 70s. I had a four-foot birdie putt to shoot 75. No matter how happy I was to shoot a 77, I still wonder how in the world I three-putted from 4 feet. Of course it had nothing to do with my stroke; from the second I walked off the green until today, I keep talking about the pressure involved with shooting that first round in the 70's and how that pressure, and not my shaky putting stroke cost me a 75. So, whether you are lining up a 2 footer or a 32 footer, if the putt will have any impact on an important scoring milestone, be sure to let everyone around you know that you are gunning for a personal best, no one will ever question that the nerves got to you; and, if you make it, then you are clutch under pressure and your playing partners will be even more impressed.

*D. Lessons*

We have all heard the saying "Practice makes perfect" myriad times in our life and for the most part this is absolutely true. The one exception might very well be the round of golf immediately following a lesson.

A few years ago I took a three-hole playing lesson with the club pro at Sea Oaks. On the last hole of the lesson I hooked my drive into the woods on a long Par-5. Before I got ready to punch out into the fairway leaving myself 290 yards to the hole, he asked why I would settle for being nearly 300 yards away when I could be 120 yards and then went on to show me how to play a dramatic low hook. I executed it perfectly. The ball flew off my club and made a left turn, ending up in the middle of the fairway 125 yards from the center of the green. I made my par and realized that I had just played those three holes at 1-under. Pumped at the end of this lesson, I decided to play 9-holes and use my new-found skills to shoot a course record 29. Unfortunately, it did not go quite as I planned.

Lessons may help your game in the end, but for the first few rounds after a lesson, there is no doubt that you will struggle. Make it known to all within earshot that you just took a lesson and the instructor gave you so many swing thoughts that you are just trying to digest and implement them. We have all been there, so no one will doubt you. A good little trick to bolster this excuse is to keep a little piece of paper in your pocket. After each poor shot, take it out and study it. When your playing partners ask you what the paper is, just tell them that your instructor gave you a few key swing thoughts to keep in mind. Be careful here, you need to have a piece of paper with actual golf points written on it just in case someone either looks over your shoulder or asks to see it. Remember, it's called commitment.

## 9. GENDER SPECIFIC

Women have a lot of power that men don't have, key among them (for purposes of this book at least) is the ability to formulate an excuse based on their gender. Now, before we get into these excuses, let me state a couple of things for the record: (1) I have a mother and a wife both of whom I love very much; (2) all of these excuses were given to me by one of these women or one of their friends; (3) these stories are told to you either as they were told to me or, in one case, as I observed on my own; and (4) writing these excuses here does not mean that men are pigs, we are pigs regardless (according to my wife).

*A. Women's Clothing*

This one comes care of my mother. She called me one day after she had just finished a particularly poor round of golf. When I answered the phone, the first thing she said to me was "I have a new excuse for the book you're working on. My bra wire ruined my game today." I responded as I imagine most men would, "Umm, okay, sure. What the heck are you talking about?" She proceeded to inform me that the bra she wore for that day's round broke and the wire kept pinching her skin every time she swung. You know what; I am just as uncomfortable writing that now as I was hearing it the first time. Let's just move on, shall we? Suffice it to say, that women, if you have special clothing (bras, sports bras, thongs) that could potentially get in the way or affect your swing, make sure to share them with your group. And, if you are playing with men they will either (a) be so uncomfortable that they will not call you on it or (b) be so turned on that they won't realize you are actually using it as an excuse.

*B. Boobs in the way*

I tried, unsuccessfully, to teach my wife how to golf. Now I know a lot of you are thinking, "Are you crazy trying to teach your wife to golf? That's a recipe for disaster." Well two things: first, it was her idea, and second I never tried to teach her, I just got her lessons and stayed out of the way. After the first lesson she took, I asked her how it went. Her response was short and to the point, "My boobs kept getting in the way. I don't know how your mom plays this game." The moral: women, feel free to use your breasts as an excuse in any form you desire. Maybe they are too big and they get in the way, or maybe they are too small and you were thinking about implants during your swing. Maybe you had an itch on one and it distracted you. Regardless, not one man on God's green Earth would be dumb enough to question you if you use your breasts as an excuse for a poor golf shot…we may be dumb, but we are not THAT dumb.

*C. Pregnant*

This is actually quite a remarkable story and proof of just how much some people love golf. I went out to play golf late one summer afternoon by myself. I ended up getting grouped with a husband and wife, and the wife was pregnant. Not just a month or two pregnant, but 8 months! She had a huge belly (note, I did not say she was fat, I would never say that). Somehow she had actually managed to make a relatively normal swing and it was a pretty nice swing at that. She played the first two holes bogey-bogey. Everything was going great until she mishit her drive on the third hole. That's when her (dumb) husband said, "Honey, you lifted your head up there." Her response was one of an all time classic and one of my favorite lines I have ever heard on a golf course, "Why don't you shut up, I'm carrying your baby, so really you're the reason I missed that shot." He said nothing; what could he say? For the rest of the round, every time she missed a shot, she would just look at him, point at her belly and say "Your baby, your fault." I never laughed so hard.

So ladies, the lesson here is if you are pregnant, just blame us. We did this to you and we are not nearly dumb enough to call you out if you use the "Your baby, your fault" logic as an excuse. Just one word of advice: make sure you are pregnant, because if you try to use this line and you're not pregnant, then your husband gets to use the "You just gave me a heart attack" excuse.

D. *That time of the month*

On second thought, I am not touching this subject.

## 10. CONCLUSION

So what have we learned from reading this book? First and foremost, always keep your eyes and ears open because good excuses are out there, you just need to find them. Second, when using an excuse, believability is the most important feature. And finally, just like you must do with your shot choice, it is imperative to commit to your excuse, no matter how asinine it might end up being. In the words of that great 20$^{th}$ century philosopher, George Costanza, "It's not really a lie if YOU believe it."

Well, I hope you have enjoyed reading this book as much as I enjoyed writing it. Looking back on these stories makes me realize just how much fun golf can be and I hope you all remember not to take it too seriously, because at the end of the day it is just a game. Of course, if you do decide to take it seriously, just remember, that can be an excuse as well.